TREASURES FROM AUSTRALIAN CHURCHES

Judith O'Callaghan

Curator of Metalwork
National Gallery of Victoria

This exhibition and catalogue have been generously
supported by the Crafts Board of the Australia Council.

Published by the National Gallery of Victoria
180 St Kilda Road, Melbourne, 1985

O'Callaghan, Judith 1954 –.
  Treasures from Australian churches.

  Bibliography.
  1SBN 0 7241 0110 1.

  1. Church plate, Australian – Exhibitions I. National
  Gallery of Victoria. II. Title.

739.2

National Gallery of Victoria
4 September – 5 November 1985

Cover illustration
cat no. 49

Editor:Judith Ryan
Designer: Kathy Richards
Photography: Sue McNab
Typesetting: National Gallery of Victoria
Printing: Tripart Marketing Pty Ltd

CONTENTS

4   Acknowledgements

5   Foreword

6   List of Lenders

7   Preface

9   Introduction

11   The Nineteenth Century

14   The Twentieth Century
The Arts and Crafts Movement
The Trade Manufacturers
Craftworkers since the 1940s

30   Catalogue

64   Bibliography

ACKNOWLEDGEMENTS

I am greatly indebted to the churches, communities and individuals who have lent works to the exhibition and allowed them to be reproduced in the catalogue. Their support and generosity have been outstanding. I am particularly grateful to those parishes that have made special arrangements to accommodate the absence of pieces normally in constant use.

I would also like to acknowledge the substantial contribution of the Crafts Board of the Australia Council towards both the exhibition and catalogue. Many people rendered valuable assistance during the course of my research. I wish to thank in particular: Brian Andrews, Br. L.J. Ansell C.F.C., Robert Bell, Barry Egan, Thomas Hazell, Rev. Father G.H. Jarrett, John Linton, Caroline Miley, Win Murdoch, Richard Phillips, Max Potter, Dick Richards, Peter Roberts, Iris Rossen, Geoffrey Stilwell, Patricia Summerfield, Judith Thompson, as well as the relatives of various craftworkers who supplied important biographical information—and, of course, the craftworkers themselves. I am also indebted to Glennys Wild of the Birmingham City Art Gallery, Eric Turner of the Victoria and Albert Museum, London, Robert Baines and Kay Leah.

Within the National Gallery of Victoria, special thanks are due to Janet Brady, Typesetter, Anne Cotter-Ross, Exhibitions Conservator, Tom Dixon, Senior Conservator, Richard Glover, Acting Exhibitions Officer, Elizabeth Krstevska, Typist, Margaret Legge, Curator of Ceramics and Antiquities, Sue McNab, Photographer, Gordon Morrison, Registrar, Kathy Richards, Graphic Designer, Judith Ryan, Editor and Helen Skuse, Assistant Photographer.

Judith O'Callaghan
Curator of Metalwork

FOREWORD

Throughout its history, the church has been one of the great patrons of Western art. The grand architectural imagery of the church—the New Temple, House of God, Palace of the Virgin and so on—has required an equally sumptuous decoration of the interior. It has bred some of the greatest cycles of paintings and the most moving sculptures in European art, extending to the furniture of the church—the pulpit and altar, choir stall and pew—right down to the liturgical vestments of the clergy. And amongst the richest and most potent of all objects produced within the frame of the Christian church is its metalware —chalice and paten, altar lamp and candlestick, processional cross and decorated lectern.

It may come as a surprise to some that the Australian churches with their much shorter history should share in this rich inheritance. Judith O'Callaghan, Curator of Metalwork at the National Gallery of Victoria, is to be congratulated on her exhibition and catalogue which focus for the first time on this important aspect of Australia's heritage. Miss O'Callaghan traces a pattern of dependence on revivalist styles emanating from Victorian England : the Ecclesiological Society which influenced colonial Anglican ecclesiastical practice and James Hardman and Co. which had a particular influence over Roman Catholic liturgical design. As the 20th century gathered pace however, so did the independence and innovation of Australian designers and makers, reflecting the broader pattern of Australian cultural life.

The National Gallery of Victoria is most grateful to those churches who, for the time of the exhibition, have deprived themselves of their treasures and shared them so generously with a wider public. It would not have been possible for the Gallery to have mounted this, the first museum exhibition of these treasures or prepared the scholarly catalogue without the generous support of the Crafts Board of the Australia Council and it gratefully acknowledges its willing assistance in this important project.

Patrick McCaughey
Director
National Gallery of Victoria

LIST OF LENDERS

All Saints' Anglican Church, Geelong, Victoria
All Saints' Anglican Church, Greensborough, Victoria
Anglican Church of the Epiphany, Crafers, South Australia
Anglican Diocese of Adelaide
Catholic Diocese of Ballarat, Victoria
Catholic Diocese of Melbourne
Catholic Diocesan Archives, Toowoomba, Queensland
Christ Church Anglican Cathedral, Newcastle, New South Wales
Congregational Church, Pitt Street, Sydney (now the Uniting Church)
Holy Trinity Anglican Cathedral, Wangaratta, Victoria
J. Klinger Esq., Adelaide
John Linton Esq., Maylands, Western Australia
John Linton Esq., Perth
Mary Immaculate Catholic Church, Ivanhoe, Victoria
Miss K. Sargison, Hobart
Mrs B. Flynn, Kyneton, Victoria
Pius XII Provincial Seminary, Banyo, Queensland
Port Keats Catholic Church, Northern Territory
Pulteney Grammar School, Adelaide
Reverend Christopher Ross, O.S.M., Perth
Sacred Heart Catholic Cathedral, Bendigo, Victoria
Scots Church, Sydney
Society of the Sacred Advent, Brisbane
St Andrew's Anglican Church, Brighton, Victoria
St Anselm's Anglican Church, Middle Park, Victoria
St Boniface's Anglican Cathedral, Bunbury, Western Australia
St David's Anglican Cathedral, Hobart
St Dennis' Catholic Church, Joondanna, Western Australia
St Francis Xavier Catholic Cathedral, Adelaide

St George's Anglican Church, East Ivanhoe, Victoria
St George's Anglican Cathedral, Perth
St Joseph's Catholic Church, Leeton, New South Wales
St Jude's Anglican Church, Brighton, South Australia
St Mary's College, University of Melbourne
St Mary's Catholic Cathedral, Sydney
St Mary's Catholic Cathedral, Hobart
St Mark's Anglican Church, Camberwell, Victoria
St Patrick's Catholic Cathedral, Melbourne
St Patrick's Catholic Church, Brisbane
St Paul's Anglican Church, Bridgetown, Western Australia
St Peter's Anglican Church, East Melbourne
St Paul's Anglican Cathedral, Melbourne
St Stephen's Catholic Cathedral, Brisbane
The Anglican Parish of Mt Barker
The Anglican Parish of Christ Church, Claremont, Western Australia
The Church of the Resurrection, Macedon Ranges, Victoria
The Most Reverend Francis Patrick Carroll, Archbishop of Canberra and Goulburn
The Most Reverend Thomas F. Little, Archbishop of Melbourne
The Reverend Gary Priest, Bunbury, Western Australia
The Reverend Ian F. Brown, Melbourne
The Reverend Andrew St John, Melbourne
The Right Reverend Peter Hollingworth, Bishop of the Inner City, Melbourne Diocese
The Society of Saint Francis, Brisbane
Victoria College, Burwood Campus
Wentworth Memorial Church, Sydney
Western Australian Museum

PREFACE

Medieval England was rich in church plate, of which very little survives. The inventories drawn up by the commissioners at the time of the Reformation make depressing reading when it is realized just how many treasures were sacrificed to officially sanctioned greed. The religious revival of the 19th century occasioned a reawakening of interest in the medieval craftsmanship used in the service of the church, particularly under the enthusiastic guidance of Augustus Welby Pugin. Hand in hand with the Gothic Revival and the Oxford Movement, manufacturing companies sprang up to supply the enormous demand for ecclesiastical plate, both at home and abroad. Works of great quality were produced but the true flowering of the Gothic Revival was ever so brief; names such as Pugin and Butterfield disappeared into obscurity and the work of the craftsmen of the movement tended to be disparaged and neglected.

During the 1950s, a revival of interest in Victorian and Edwardian decorative arts led to the first-ever exhibitions in London of church plate covering the period 1830 to 1918. The evolution of style from the somewhat debased Gothic, of 18th century inspiration, to the products of the Victorian 'medievalists', largely followers of Pugin and Morris, was clearly shown and an appreciation of the best of 19th and early 20th century ecclesiastical design was established.

It would have been a relatively easy though admittedly large-scale undertaking for this exhibition in the National Gallery of Victoria to have been built on the scholarly foundations laid by the Victoria and Albert Museum and the Victorian Society, amongst others. The use of such an approach would have resulted in a truly remarkable collection of works of great quality and beauty, reflecting the religious impulses of Victorian Britain and the spirituality of the age.

Instead, and very properly so, Judith O'Callaghan has concentrated on ecclesiastical metalwork produced exclusively in Australia for Australian churches in the 19th and 20th centuries. This exhibition, the first of its kind in this country, presents a comprehensive selection of items specifically intended for the service of God in Christian churches. They range from the work of immigrant craftsmen, commissioned by immigrant clergy, varying but little from the work of their English contemporaries, to later works which are exclusively Australian in design and commission. In all a high degree of quality and commitment, both on the part of the craftsman and the donor, is very evident. The Australian parallel to the religious fervour of Victorian and Edwardian Britain, expressed in these tangible objects, is strikingly followed through, from the ecclesiological perfection of Pugin-inspired work to the uninhibited expressionism of the modern movement.

I have never seen any suggestion in 19th century Australian art and architectural criticism that the transplantion of British revived medieval styles to the colonies might be incongruous, or that these styles might be unsuitable for such changed circumstances. Be that as it may, an Australian element does begin to manifest itself gradually in stylistic evolution, both in building and artefacts, as this exhibition clearly shows.

Ecclesiastical plate seems to claim the attention of many collectors in Australia at the present time. In asking ourselves why this is so, I would suggest two possible answers. In the first place, there is perhaps a recognition that such works possess a special quality, by virtue of their purpose. The second answer might be found in the meticulous craftsmanship and attention to detail evident in so much of the design and manufacture of the metalware. Judith O'Callaghan is to be congratulated in assembling this rich and varied collection of ecclesiastical metalware in Australia which is illustrative not only of the work of superb craftsmen but also of a society which encouraged artistic endeavour and was willing to extend the traditions of patronage.

Thomas Hazell

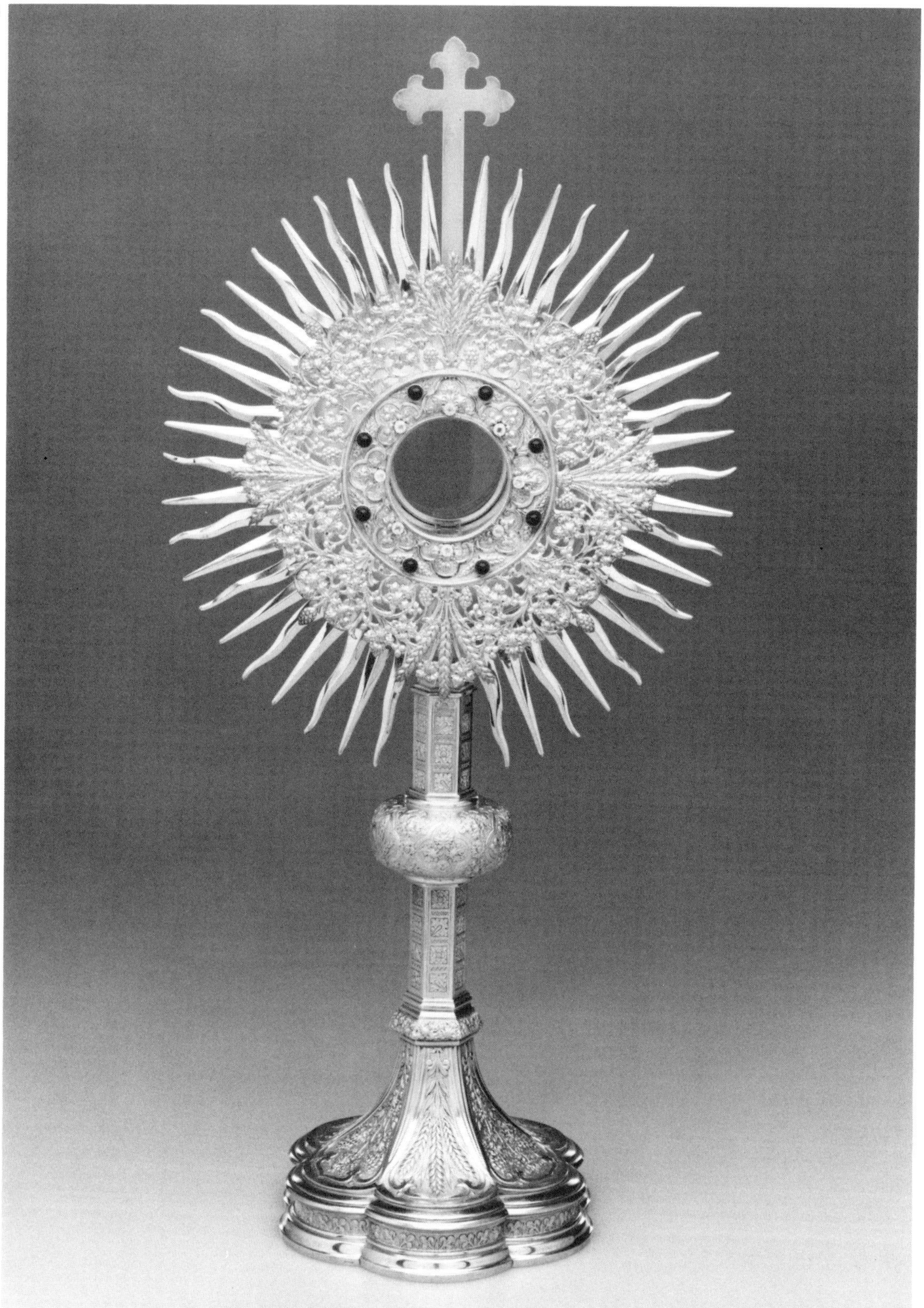

INTRODUCTION

Treasures from Australian Churches focuses exclusively on ecclesiastical metalware produced by Australian makers. Since the 19th century, the churches have constituted one of the most active sources of commission for metalworkers within this country. The seriousness of purpose attached to this type of commission promotes an emphasis on excellence rather than economy of means, offering the craftworker the opportunity to achieve an exceptional standard of design and manufacture.

Of course not every Australian church contains a sumptuous array of artefacts crafted in metal. As in the Baptist Church, this may be an expression of denominational preference, yet in recent years there have been moves towards a studied simplicity even within those denominations with a rich tradition of ritual, such as the Catholic Church. It is still the concern of patrons, however, to maintain the quality of those objects and fittings appropriate to their form of worship, and metalworkers are commissioned accordingly.

Ecclesiastical commissions have various origins. They may relate specifically to the furnishing of a new church or the refurbishment of an older one. Alternatively, they may be of a distinctly personal nature, for example, memorials, thank offerings or commemorations of ordinations. Frequently they celebrate an important event in the history of a parish. For example, the elaborate solid gold chalice set with precious stones made by T. Gaunt & Co. in 1941 (cat. 23) commemorates the centenary of St Francis' Church, the first Catholic church in Melbourne. Gold and jewellery were donated by 'benefactors and friends' of the church to provide the materials necessary to make the chalice, a common practice amongst Australian congregations.

There are also public memorials, perhaps the most outstanding being the Warriors' Chapel in Christ Church Anglican Cathedral, Newcastle. The chapel and all its fittings were created in the 1920s as a monument to the men of the Newcastle Diocese who had been killed in the first world war. The extensive metalware commission for the chapel included altar cross, candlesticks, vases, chalice and paten, altar lamp, alms dish, a bronze depicting the crucifixion and an illuminated book, encased in gold, recording each soldier's name. (The work was carried out by Melbourne maker William Mark, see cat. 45–47). Numerous commissions to commemorate the war dead have provided furnishings for churches throughout Australia.

Ultimately the quality of an ecclesiastical commission relates to the spirit of commitment associated with the making of a religious offering. The skill of the craftworker and the oblation of the patron are together offered to the glory of God. This is eloquently expressed in the following report in *The Adelaide Times* of 1856 recording the acquisition of a communion service (cat. 2) by the Anglican parish of Blakiston:

> The congregation of St. James's Church … are now furnished with an excellent service of communion plate. It is generally agreed that the maker, Mr. Firnhaber, has displayed both skill and taste in the chasing and symmetry of his work; whilst the appearance and value of the plate itself will not be an unfit illustration of the sentiment, which should find a response in every Christian heart, 'I will not offer unto the Lord my God that which doth cost me nothing'.[1]

1. *The Adelaide Times*, 22 January 1856. Mr Richard Phillips kindly provided this reference.

1

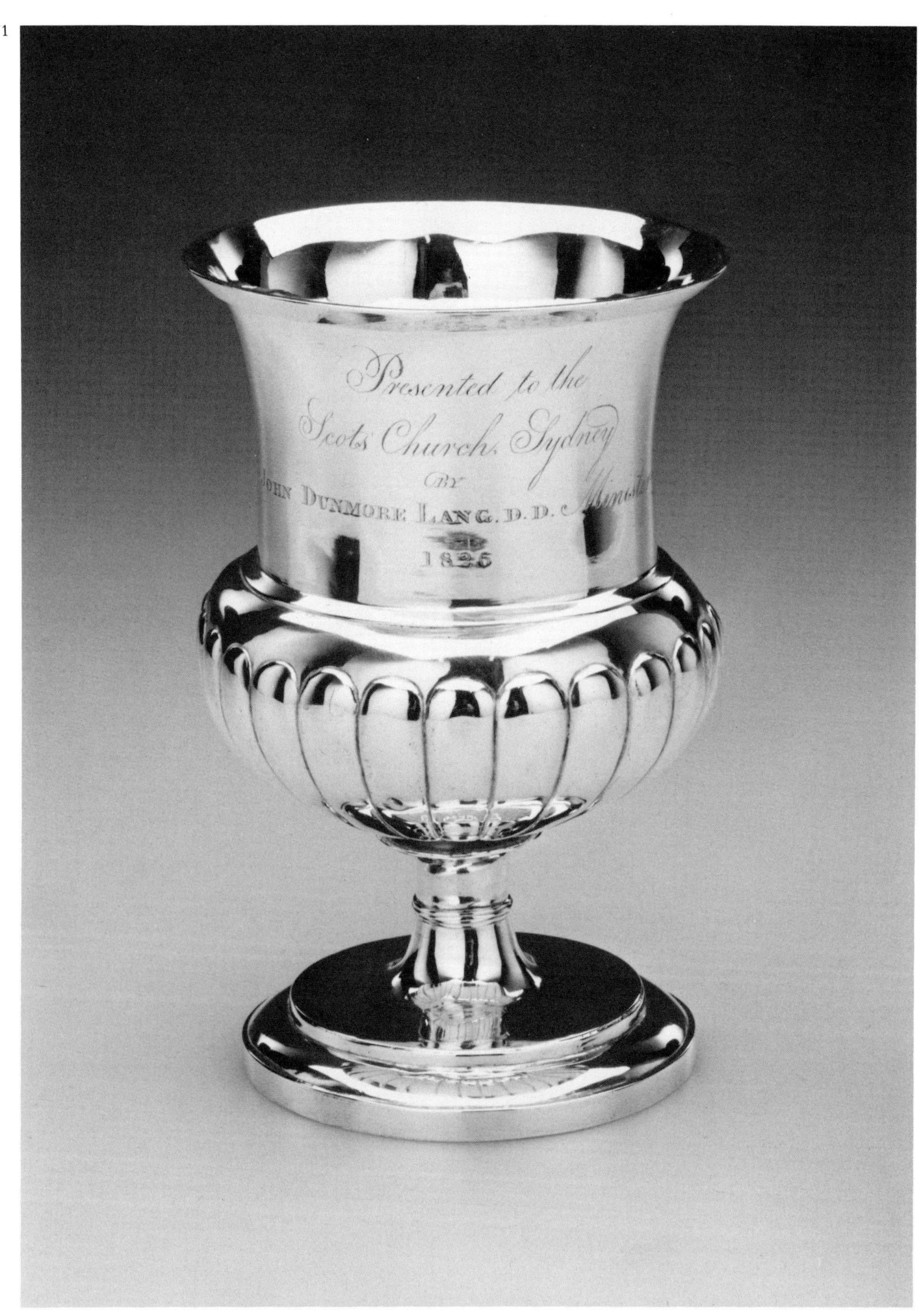

Presented to the
Scots Church, Sydney
By
JOHN DUNMORE LANG. D.D. Minister
1825

THE NINETEENTH CENTURY

The handsome Regency style chalice bearing the maker's mark of James Robertson of Sydney (cat. 1)[2] represents the earliest known ecclesiastical commission of colonial manufacture. The chalice is one of a pair commissioned by the Reverend John Dunmore Lang for presentation to Scots Church, Sydney in 1826.

Ecclesiastical metalwork executed by local makers during these early years of European settlement appears to have been the exception rather than the rule. Churches were generally furnished with imported wares. Many were presentation gifts, some of royal origin such as the communion service at St David's Cathedral, Hobart, which has the dedicatory inscription: 'This Service of Communion Plate was presented by HIS MAJESTY KING GEORGE the 3rd for use of the Chapel at HIS MAJESTY'S Settlement at Port Phillip, Bass's Streights in New South Wales, 1803'. Bearing witness to the vagaries of circumstance, the service arrived with the first settlers at Port Phillip Bay in 1803 but departed with them to Tasmania when the settlement failed. George III also presented a communion service to St Phillip's Church, Sydney in 1803, while William IV presented services to St James' Church and St Andrew's Cathedral, Sydney.[3]

The furnishing of many colonial Anglican churches owed much to an English foundation, the Cambridge Camden (later Ecclesiological) Society. The Society, which was set up in 1839 'to promote the study of Ecclesiastical Architecture and Antiquities, and the restoration of mutilated architectural remains',[4] dictated the visual style of the liturgical and ceremonial revival which took place in the Church of England, last century. The Society took a distinct interest in the progress of church building and decoration in the colonies, featuring reports on the latest developments in its periodical, *The Ecclesiologist*. Many of these were provided by members of the Society living in Australia, such as the Reverend W.H. Walsh of Sydney and the Reverend F.H. Cox of Tasmania. Between 1844 and 1847 the Society published

Instrumenta Ecclesiastica which contained 'a variety of working drawings of details and fittings appertaining to churches and their precincts',[5] stated to be 'chiefly undertaken for the sake of the Colonies'.[6] The designs, based on medieval models, were supplied by the architect William Butterfield (1814–1900), a committed Gothic revivalist who was later to provide plans for the Cathedral Church of St Peter, Adelaide and St Paul's Cathedral, Melbourne.[7]

There are many Anglican churches in Australia which hold examples of the recommended style of plate. These usually bear the maker's mark of John Keith of London, the silversmithing firm patronized by the Society. There are, however, notable examples of locally made communion plate which adhere to the designs illustrated in the *Instrumenta Ecclesiastica*—for instance, the very fine chalice and paten (fig. 1)[8] by South Australian silversmith Henry Steiner, held at the Cathedral Church of St Peter. Moreover these duplicate exactly, with the exception of the paten's legend, the chalice and paten by John Keith, dated 1847–48, also belonging to the Cathedral.[9] Yet another two chalices and patens of exactly the same design, as well as a complementary wine flagon, can be found at Christ Church Anglican Parish, one of the oldest in Adelaide and in very close proximity to the Cathedral. These pieces, with the exception of one paten, bear the mark of Charles Firnhaber, another prominent South Australian maker.

The early Catholic churches looked to another source of 'correct' ecclesiastical design—the Birmingham firm of John Hardman and Co., which by the mid-1840s could supply not only an extensive range of plate and metal fittings but also stained glass. Hardman's designs were in the 'true' style of Gothic as propounded by A.W.N. Pugin (1812–52), the great polemicist of the English Gothic Revival. Pugin had been instrumental in establishing the firm in 1838 and was its chief designer until his death in 1852. He also had many connnections with the Catholic

---

2. Hawkins 1973, p.15. Hawkins maintains that Alexander Dick, who apparently worked for Robertson between 1824 and 1826, was the actual maker.
3. Grimwade 1947, pp.100–02; Hawkins 1980, pp.78–81.
4. 'Laws of the Cambridge Camden Society, (from Report of the Cambridge Camden Society for MDCCCXLII, pp.44–6) as published

in White 1962, p.225, Appendix A.
5. The Ecclesiological late Cambridge Camden Society (ed.), *Instrumenta Ecclesiastica* First Series , John van Voorst, London, 1847.
6. 'Report of the Thirty-seventh Meeting of the Cambridge Camden Society on Tuesday, April 30, 1844', *The Ecclesiologist* xxxi. xxxii., p.117, May 1844.
7. Neither cathedral was completed to Butterfield's specifications.

8. *Instrumenta Ecclesiastica* 1847, plate LV —'Chalices and Patens'.
9. The paten accompanying the Keith chalice actually bears Steiner's mark. This may be explained by the existence of a Keith paten at Christ Church used with one of the Firnhaber chalices. Obviously the patens have been interchanged at some point. Probably the Steiner paten was commissioned as a replacement for one by Firnhaber.

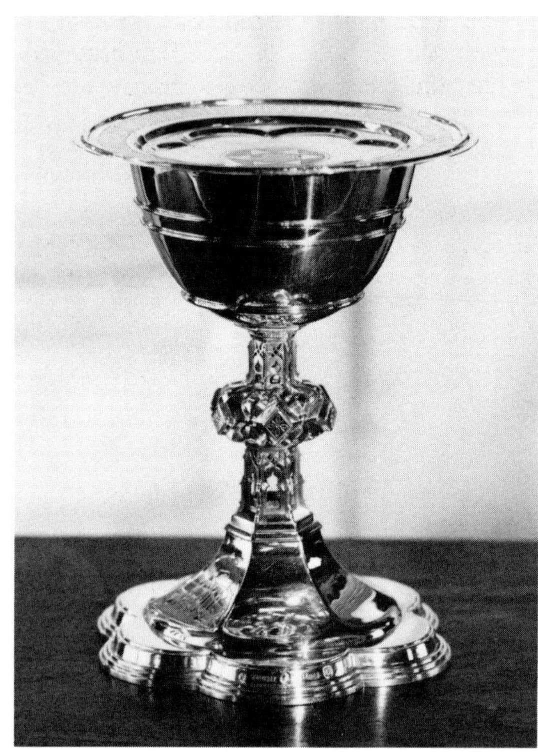

fig. 1
Chalice and paten c1880 by Henry Steiner (photograph courtesy of The Flinders University of South Australia)

clergy in Australia, particularly with Bishop Willson of Hobart to whom quantities of church furnishings by Hardman's were sent in the 1840s.[10] Certainly Hardman's Day Books are scattered with orders from Australia dating from the early 1840s right through the 19th century. Some were supplied directly to the clergy, others via colonial architects such as William Wilkinson Wardell (1823–99), designer of St Patrick's Cathedral, Melbourne and St Mary's Cathedral, Sydney.

Overseas imports were not confined to English sources. Irish, Italian and particularly French wares were imported in abundance. These imported wares varied considerably in type and quality, ranging from stock items of conventional design and small intrinsic value, to high quality replicas of early ecclesiastical treasures. In one outstanding case, an entire altar in brass, complete with seven statues, was imported from France for St Patrick's Catholic Church, Sydney. As seen earlier, some of these imports provided the models for local

makers, but such copying was not restricted to English wares. A pair of silver-gilt chalices made by William Edwards of Melbourne in 1866 (cat. 3) and an earlier 19th century French chalice, located at St Francis' Catholic Church, Melbourne, are too close in design and decoration for the resemblance to be fortuitous.

Like most of the colonial silversmiths represented in this exhibition, Robertson, Firnhaber, Edwards and Steiner were not known specifically as ecclesiastical makers. They received this type of commission because of their reputations as gold and silversmiths. Naturally it was not uncommon for a maker to be closely associated with a church. Edward Hollingdale of Sydney, for example, who made the splendid gold crozier (cat. 11) for presentation to Archbishop Vaughan in 1877, was a strong supporter of the Catholic Church and treasurer of the St Mary's Cathedral Building Fund for many years.[11]

There were others, like John McLean of Sydney and Denis Brothers of Melbourne, who advertised ecclesiastical wares amongst their other lines. Denis Brothers was obviously well known for its church work and was called upon to supply many important commissions such as the gold chalice presented to Bishop Reville in 1885 (cat. 7). By the 1890s the firm was advertising regularly in *The Advocate*, the Catholic newspaper for Melbourne, and, although the earlier advertisements only refer to a range of imported ecclesiastical wares, by 1897 the description had been amplified to 'Importers of Vestments and all Church Requisites. Manufacturers of Gold and Silver Chalices, Ciboriums, Monstrances, Oilstocks, Pyxes &c., &c., Only Artistic Designers and Experienced Workmen employed'.[12]

The main competition to Denis Brothers would have been T. Gaunt & Co. of Melbourne, which was well established by the 1890s as a leading manufacturer of ecclesiastical wares. The business was founded by Thomas Gaunt in 1856 and survived, under various changes of management, until 1979 when its workshop finally closed. It also offered a range of secular wares, but its main line was definitely 'CHURCH REQUISITES. Silver, brass or Electroplated Churchware Made to Order on the Premises'.[13] The architect William Wardell is known to have worked with the firm to provide metalwork for St Patrick's

10. Hardman's Day Books, April, October, November, December 1843; January 1844 and December 1847, located at the Birmingham City Art Gallery.
11. Hawkins 1973, p.44.
12. *The Advocate*, 30 October 1897, advertisement in the Supplement.
13. *The Advocate*, 16 December 1893, advertisement.

Cathedral, Melbourne, although not to the extent that is traditionally held. Most of the metal fittings and furniture, particularly that of the high altar and sanctuary, appear to have been supplied by Hardman's of Birmingham.[14] However Wardell did design some items of brassware which bear Gaunt's mark and,[15] according to a report in *The Advocate* of October 1897 publicizing the opening of the Cathedral, 'With one or two exceptions the whole of the altar plate, in gold, silver, and brass, has been made by Messrs. T. Gaunt and Co., of this city. It includes a large monstrance in gold and silver, weighing nearly 100 oz' (cat. 18). It is also noted that 'Apart from the altar furniture, the same firm have made the beautiful pectoral cross and chain which his Grace the Archbishop wears daily [cat. 17]. It is a very massive cross of pure gold, set with emeralds and diamonds on the front. The crucifixion is handsomely chased, while the reverse is engraved with vines and wheat.'[16] This cross may have been designed by Wardell. Unlike Denis Brothers, which closed around 1910, Gaunt's flourished well into the 20th century, supplying the requirements of churches throughout Victoria and Australia.

14. Hardman's Day Books, June, July 1869, June 1897.
15. de Jong 1983, p.79, cat. 138, 139.
16. *The Advocate*, 30 October 1897, p.16.

THE TWENTIETH CENTURY

THE ARTS AND CRAFTS MOVEMENT

The British Arts and Crafts movement exerted a strong influence on Australian metalworkers during the early years of the 20th century and served to establish the idea of the 'artist craftsman' in this country. The main impetus of the movement was the desire to exalt the craftworker and to counteract the ill effects of mechanization on craft production subsequent to the industrial revolution. To this end, its followers emphasized truth to materials and honest, that is self-evident methods of construction. In metalwork, the style was characterized by handbeaten surfaces, the use of non-precious metals, enamelwork and cabochon-cut semi-precious stones. The movement was essentially medievalist, looking back to a time when the craftsman was both designer and maker, and these features were meant to imitate elements of medieval metalcraft. The association between medieval style and correct ecclesiastical design established by the leaders of the Gothic Revival earlier in the 19th century, encouraged the acceptance of the Arts and Crafts style as particularly appropriate for church wares.

A number of local metalworkers had direct contact with the British movement. These included J.W.R. Linton, Alan C. Walker, William Mark and Caroline Francis,[17] all of whom spent time in England during the early part of this century. James W.R. Linton was English born, arriving in Western Australia from London in 1896. His father was Sir James Dromgole Linton, President of the Royal Institute of Painters in Water Colours and a friend of John Ruskin. Linton had trained as an artist and architect in London and he first became known in Perth as a painter. During a return trip to London in 1907, he attended classes in metalwork, enamelling, jewellery and bronze casting at the Sir John Cass Technical Institute.[18] Harold Stabler, a leading figure in the British Arts and Crafts movement, had just been appointed Head of the Institute Art School. It would appear that he had a significant

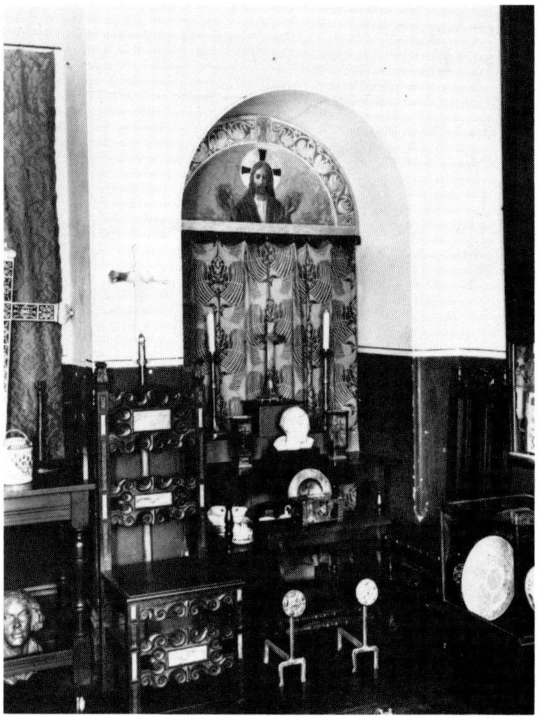

fig. 2
Contemporary photograph of craftwork display by J.W.R. Linton (courtesy of the Western Australian Museum)

influence upon Linton who described this accomplished silversmith and enamellist as 'a most generous helper'.[19]

Upon Linton's return to Perth in 1908, craft, especially metalwork assumed a major place in his *oeuvre*. Surviving drawings and photographs (fig.2) make it clear that ecclesiastical metalwork occupied much of his attention. Technically versatile, Linton's ecclesiastical wares ranged from delicately wrought chalices (cat. 26) to furniture and fittings, such as brass altar sets of cross and candlesticks (cat. 27). A comparison between Linton's chalice and one by Stabler, illustrated in *The Studio* of 1915,[20] reinforces the close connection between the two makers. The overall design bears distinct similarities to Stabler's piece but Linton has

17. Caroline Francis (cat. 51), who was a student at the National Gallery School, Melbourne and a member of the Yarra Sculptors' Society, left Australia some time after 1904. Her jewellery and enamelwork were reviewed in *The Studio* of 1925, where it states that she 'won a South Kensington diploma and silver medals, and has exhibited at the Royal Academy, the Royal Colonial Institute and the Paris Salon ... and had spent many years in Europe'. It is apparent that ecclesiastical metalwork constituted a significant part of her work. Unfortunately it is not known whether she returned to Australia.

18. Gray 1977.
19. Quoted in Moore 1934, vol. II, p.102.
20. Illustrated in Hamilton T. Smith, 'Harold Stabler, Worker in Metals and Enamels', *The Studio* XLIV, 1915, p.39.

modified the decorative elements mainly through the substitution of wire. The chalice was executed during the term of Linton's partnership with Arthur Cross, an Englishman whom he had met at the Sir John Cass Institute. Cross died in 1917 and during the early 20s, Linton's son Jamie joined his father in the workshop. Jamie's background was a mixture of fine and applied art, and in 1926 he travelled to Europe to study under Emile Antoine Bourdelle in Paris and at the Central School of Arts and Crafts, London.[21] When he returned to Western Australia in 1928, he resumed working in metal with his father while pursuing other artistic interests, particularly sculpture.

The six pieces commissioned during the 1940s by the parishioners of St Jude's Anglican Church, Brighton (cat. 57–59) illustrate a combination of talents. The designs, incorporating lightly hammered surfaces and enamelwork, are basically Arts and Crafts inspired, but streamlined to achieve a more contemporary look. A confident hand is revealed in the energetic and expressive modelling of the dolphins on the bases of the cross and candlesticks. The marine motifs of dolphins, ships and shells, replete with Christian symbolism, are most appropriate to this church located on the South Australian coast.

As the work of Jamie Linton suggests, the Arts and Crafts style persisted in Australia well into the 1940s. This is particularly evident in the work of those craftworkers who learnt their skills during the early years of the century and afterwards worked in relative isolation. Gordon Holdsworth, another Western Australian, is a pertinent example. Born in Middlesex in 1886, Holdsworth arrived in Perth in 1900, having spent time in Saudi Arabia and India on the way. Settling in the tiny village of Hester near Bridgetown, he remained there until his death in 1965.[22]

During his early years in Western Australia, Holdsworth received tuition from J.W.R. Linton, presumably during his time at the Perth Art School around the end of the first decade. This training was in painting as well as metalwork and Holdsworth continued to work in both areas throughout his life. His metalwork ranged from fine silver jewellery to large wrought iron work, such as the rood screen made for St John's Anglican Church, Albany. Despite his apparent isolation, Holdsworth managed to fabricate a large

and technically ambitious lectern that was to win a medal at the British Empire Exhibition at Wembley in 1924 (cat. 40). Although firmly rooted within the Arts and Crafts tradition, Holdsworth's ecclesiastical metalware always exhibits a highly individual approach. This is exemplified in the metropolitical cross which he made for St George's Cathedral, Perth (cat. 39). The handbeaten surfaces, predominant use of a non-precious metal, cabochon stones and enamelwork are all basic Arts and Crafts elements yet their combination, particularly that of the repousée silver panels over copper, defies categorization.

The Arts and Crafts style also flourished in Tasmania well into the second quarter of this century. Alan Cameron Walker, one of the state's most prominent architects, has been described as 'the father of the arts and crafts movement in Southern Tasmania'.[23] He was President of the Tasmanian Society for twenty-five years and his special 'hobby', as he would term it, was metalwork which he first studied in Hobart under Joseph Quarmby, an English jeweller. It seems certain that he also had direct contact with the British Arts and Crafts movement during a trip to England around 1905 when, according to family sources, he worked with the prominent silversmith and enamellist Alexander Fisher at his School of Enamelling in Warwick Gardens, Kensington (established in 1904). This is supported by a letter sent by Fisher to Walker, in which he invites the Tasmanian to visit him in London.[24] The letter bears no date, but does give the Warwick Gardens address. Moore in *The Story of Australian Art* states that Walker trained at the Guild of Handicraft in Chipping Campden,[25] but so far nothing has been uncovered to substantiate this claim.

When comparing Walker's altar cross of c.1931 (cat. 54) with one produced by Fisher around 1903,[26] a certain resemblance is discernible. Although Walker's design is less elaborate, he makes similar use of a symbolic vine branch to strengthen the visual effect of the intersecting arms. There is a striking contrast between this proudly handcrafted product of the skilled 'amateur' and the more important proportions and crisp finish of the solid gold monstrance (cat. 55) designed by Walker (fig. 3), but executed by a professional gold and silversmith, Harold Sargison. Sargison

21. 'J.R. Linton's Craftwork', *Art in Australia*, November 1935, p.49.
22. Biographical information on Gordon Holdsworth was generously provided by his relative, Mrs Marion Wardell Johnson.

23. 'Obituary', *The Mercury*, Monday, 14 December 1931, p.6; biographical information on Alan Cameron Walker was generously provided by his grand daughter, Mrs Roma Blackwood.
24. The letter is in the possession of his family.

25. Moore 1934, p.174.
26. Illustrated in *Victorian Church Art* 1971, p.156.

had also trained under Joseph Quarmby, going on to establish his own successful silversmithing business in Hobart.

Of all the Australian metalsmiths working in the style of the Arts and Crafts movement, William Mark was undoubtedly its most accomplished exponent. Mark was born in Scarsdale, Victoria in 1868 and began his career as an apprentice to J.R. Rowland, a Melbourne gold and silversmith.[27] After a short stint in South Africa, Mark travelled to England and worked for a time in Nelson Dawson's workshop before joining C.R. Ashbee's Guild of Handicraft in Chipping Campden around 1902. He was to stay in Gloucestershire for eighteen years, even after the Guild failed. During this period he received commissions from royalty, examples of his work were purchased by British museums and his fine enamelwork was featured in *The Studio*.[28]

In 1920 he returned to Australia and established a studio at his home in Gardenvale, where he remained until his death in 1956. He exhibited a number of times with the Victorian Arts and Crafts Society, receiving special mention in *The Argus* for 'a communion bread box' in the Society's exhibition of 1924.[29] Although the dimensions given are slightly different, the description fits that of a wafer box (cat. 44) now in Adelaide. This silver box, with its four turned ivory supports at each corner, delicately pierce-cut hinges and enamel medallions, is exquisitely worked. The four enamel medallions separately depict a kangaroo, dolphins, birds and fire, signifying the elements. A similar device is used to decorate the knop of the solid gold chalice (cat. 43) which Mark made to Edward Spencer's design in 1923 for St Peter's Anglican Church, East Melbourne. In this case, the four images are in the form of gold medallions.

Mark's forte was enamelwork and while at the Guild of Handicraft he and F.C. Varley were credited with introducing high quality painted enamels into the Guild's reportoire.[30] As cat. 44–49 show, he had mastered an impressive range of enamelling techniques and would frequently incorporate different ones within the same work. The splendid processional cross (cat. 49), made for St Paul's Cathedral, Melbourne to the design of Louis Williams, deserves special mention. It is set with six enamels, including four in champlevé

depicting the symbols of the Evangelists, one in cloisonné depicting the *Agnus Dei* and one in a combination of champlevé and cloisonné representing the pelican in its piety.

Ecclesiastical commissions obviously comprised a large part of Mark's production, as churches all over Australia hold examples of his fine craftsmanship. Through these commissions, particularly those of the scale and importance of Christ Church Cathedral, Newcastle, mentioned earlier, Mark was able to exercise the full range of his outstanding talents.

THE TRADE MANUFACTURERS

The 20th century has seen the emergence of a number of businesses specializing in the manufacture of ecclesiastical wares. Probably the best known throughout Australia is Pellegrini & Co.. This firm was established in Melbourne in 1890 by two Italian born brothers, Alceste and Umberto Pellegrini.[31] For the first twenty years it sold statuary, gradually extending into a line of 'Catholic goods', mostly imported from abroad. It only ventured into the manufacture of ecclesiastical plate and brassware in 1910. The firm established two workshops, one in Melbourne which specialized in silver and one in Sydney which produced brassware. These were to supply all the branches which Pellegrini & Co. established in most major cities around Australia during the first three decades of this century. Until the close of the manufacturing side of the business in recent years, many denominations took advantage of the large range of plate and furniture which Pellegrini's could offer. Like most firms, it had a stock range, but it could also work to special commissions. The simple but refined silver-gilt chalice and paten of 1948 (cat. 61) illustrate well the type of commission which Pellegrini's was most frequently called on to produce.

In competition with Pellegrini's large and imposing premises in George Street, Sydney, W.J. Sanders established a firm of 'Craftsmen in Church Plate and Art Metalwork' in 1911. Over the years its range became very extensive and included every type of church ware from oil stocks to fonts and tabernacles. Although designing most of its own work, for some time a substantial part of the firm's production has been directed towards

---

27. Biographical information on William Mark was generously provided by his daughter, Mrs J. Coleston and son, Mr W.R. Mark.

28. 'Studio-Talk', *The Studio* XLIV, 1903, pp.208–09.
29. *The Argus*, 28 March 1924, p.13.
30. Crawford 1981, see entry for William Mark.

31. For the history of Pellegrini & Co., see *Pellegrini & Co. Present This Souvenir of Their Diamond Jubilee 1890–1950*, Pellegrini & Co., Sydney, 1959.

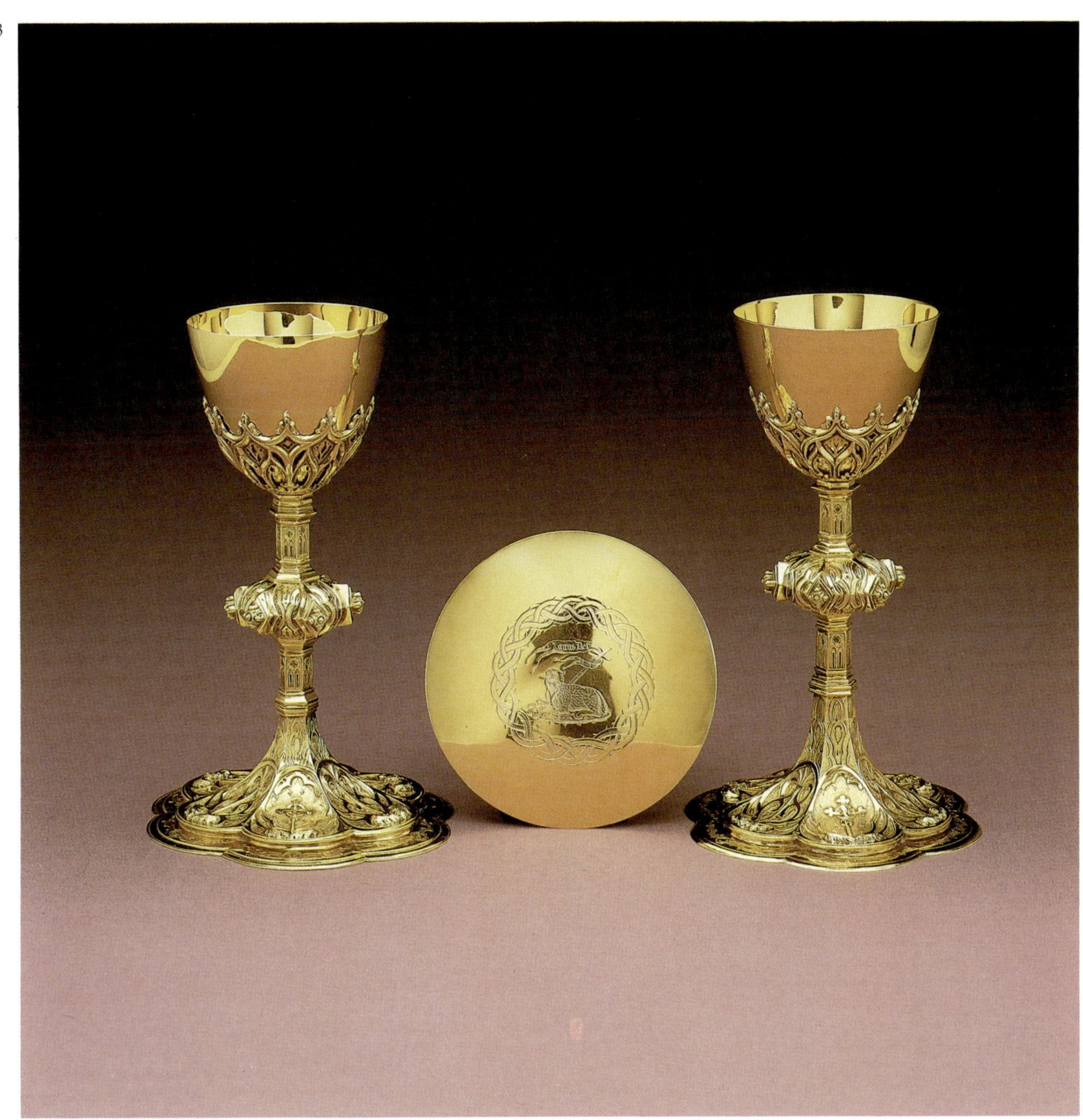

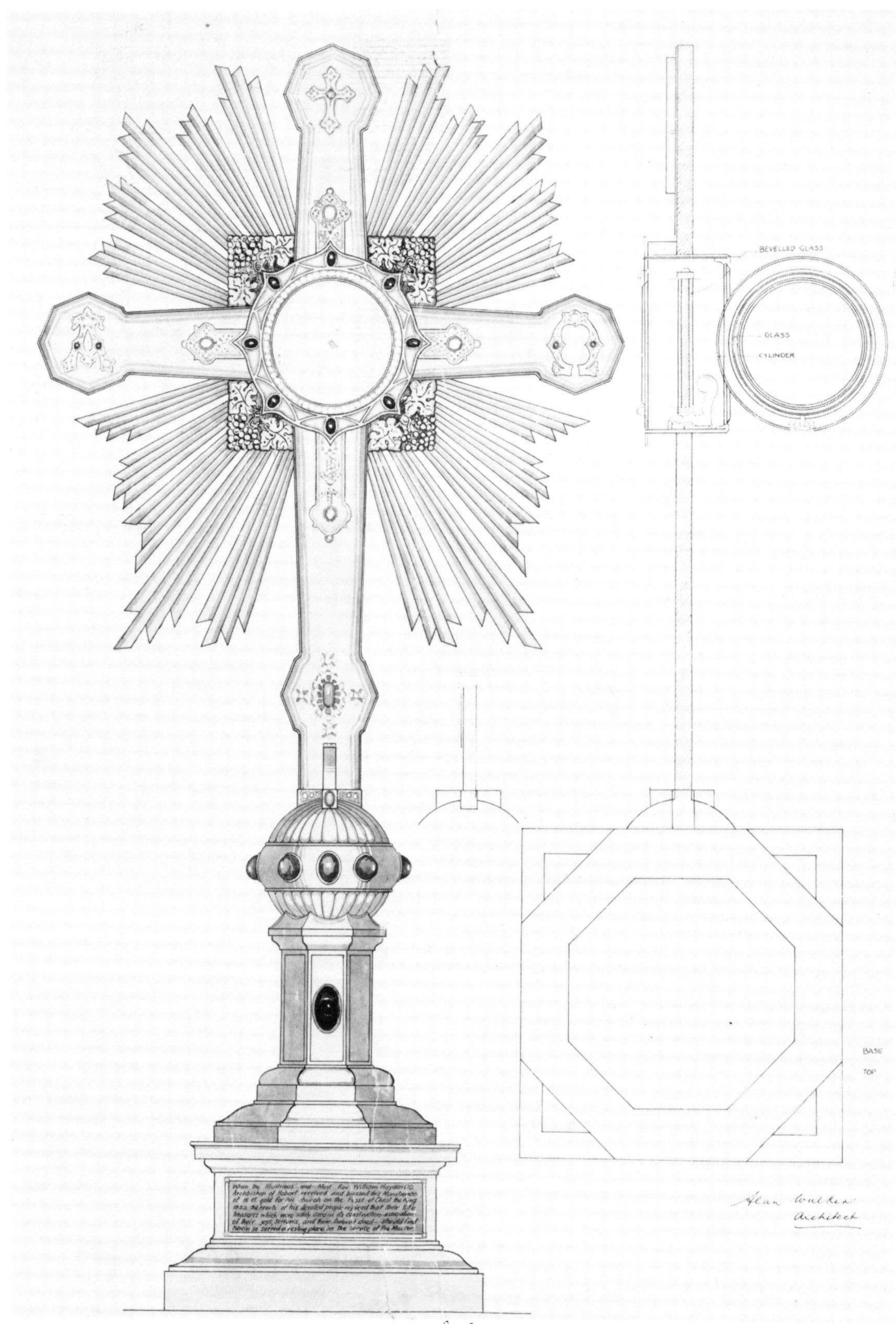

fig. 3
Design by Alan C. Walker for monstrance (cat. 55) made by
Harold Sargison (courtesy of Miss K. Sargison)

the execution of architect's designs. The dramatic sanctuary setting for St Peter Julian's Church, Sydney (fig. 4), for example, was made to the designs of Terence A. Daly, in conjunction with Stephen Moor. The firm is still in operation, although it now trades under the name of Amor-Sanders Pty Ltd.

In Queensland, F.J. Mole's has been the main local manufacturer and supplier of ecclesiastical metalwork since the business was established in 1913.[32] Its founder, Frederick James Mole, who arrived in Australia in 1910, had been involved in the metal industry in his native Birmingham. The Brisbane workshop produced a number of lines including trophies, but was best known for its 'High Class Ecclesiastical Productions of the Gold and Silversmiths Art' (fig. 5) and a range of brass church furniture. It generally received the most important local ecclesiastical commissions, including in 1928 the design and fabrication of a gold monstrance (cat. 34) intended for the Holy Name Catholic Cathedral, which was planned for Brisbane but never built. Many of Mole's designs exhibit strong stylistic characteristics, such as a bold calyx of Gothic tracery and a repeated fenestration motif decorating a faceted stem. These features can be observed in the chalice and ciborium (cat. 31, 32). The silver crozier, commissioned by the Society of the Sacred Advent for Archbishop Le Fanu of Perth in 1929 (cat. 35), presented the opportunity to develop a simple symbolic statement. Emphasizing the idea of the shepherd's crook, surface decoration was limited to a softly hammered finish, a band of chased basket-weave pattern and the appropriate coats-of-arms. F.J. Mole died in 1964, but his business survives under the management of Kevin Eager.

As in the 19th century, there were workshops that manufactured a wide range of plate but also undertook ecclesiastical work such as Levinson's in Perth (cat. 60), Fidler & Kenwrick in Adelaide (cat. 50) and J.W. Steeth & Son in Melbourne. Steeth's was probably best known for its fifty year history of making the Melbourne Cup, yet the firm also advertised as 'Specialists in Ciboria, Chalices, Remonstrances, Pyxes, Tabernacle Doors and all classes of metalwork requirements'.[33] The workshop was established by James Steeth in 1917, his son Maurice entering the business in 1945.[34] Like his father, Maurice Steeth worked as a

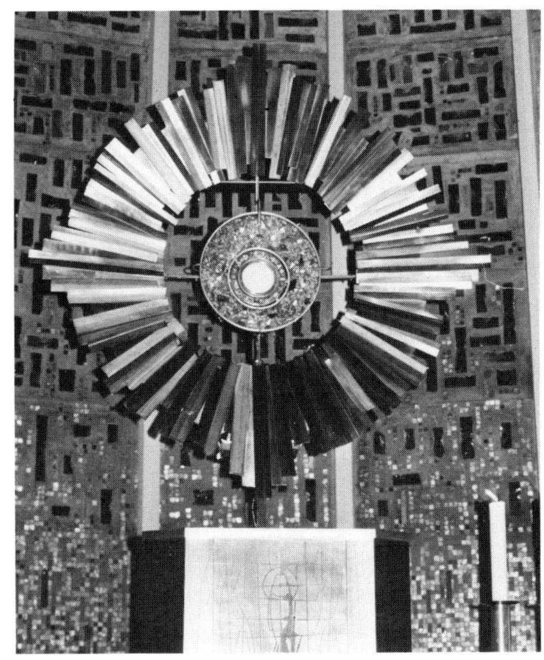

fig. 4
Detail of sanctuary furnishings c.1964 made by W.J. Sanders for St Peter Julian's Church, Sydney (photograph by Kay Leah)

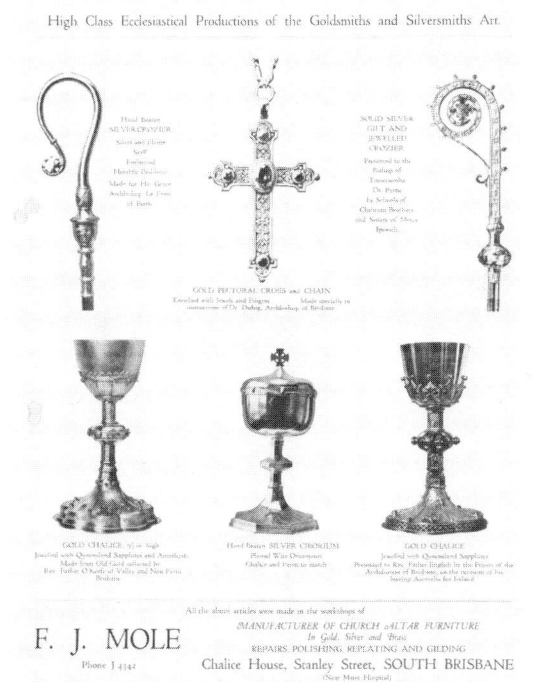

fig. 5
Page from F.J. Mole's catalogue of the 1930s illustrating cat. 35, 37, 38, 39 (note that the description below the chalice (cat. 35) is incorrect)

32. Biographical information on F.J. Mole was generously provided by his daughter, Mrs H. Cole.
33. The firm's papers, now located at University of Melbourne Archives.
34. Biographical information on Maurice Steeth was generously provided by his daughter, Ms. A. Steeth and sister, Mrs G. Lanteri.

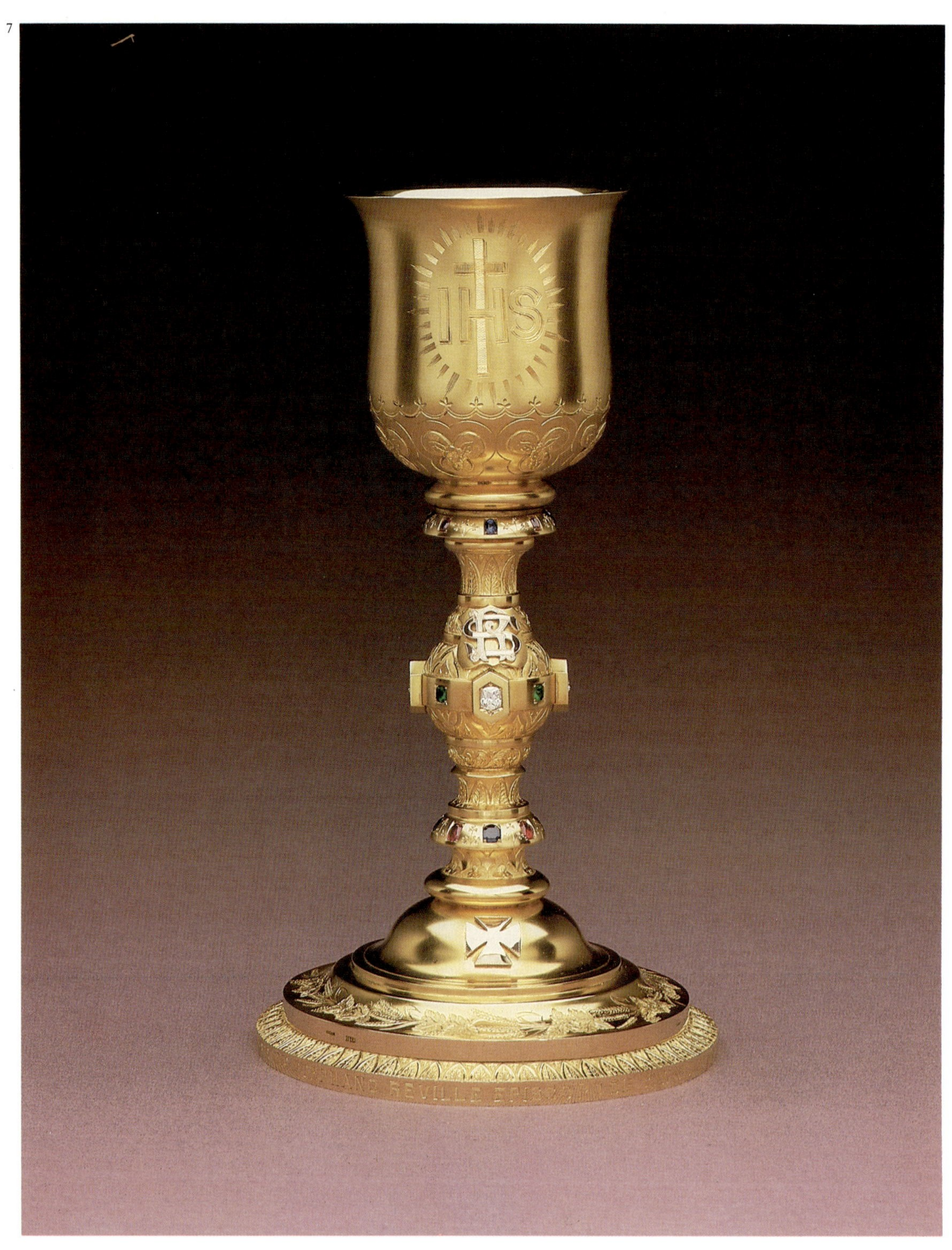

17

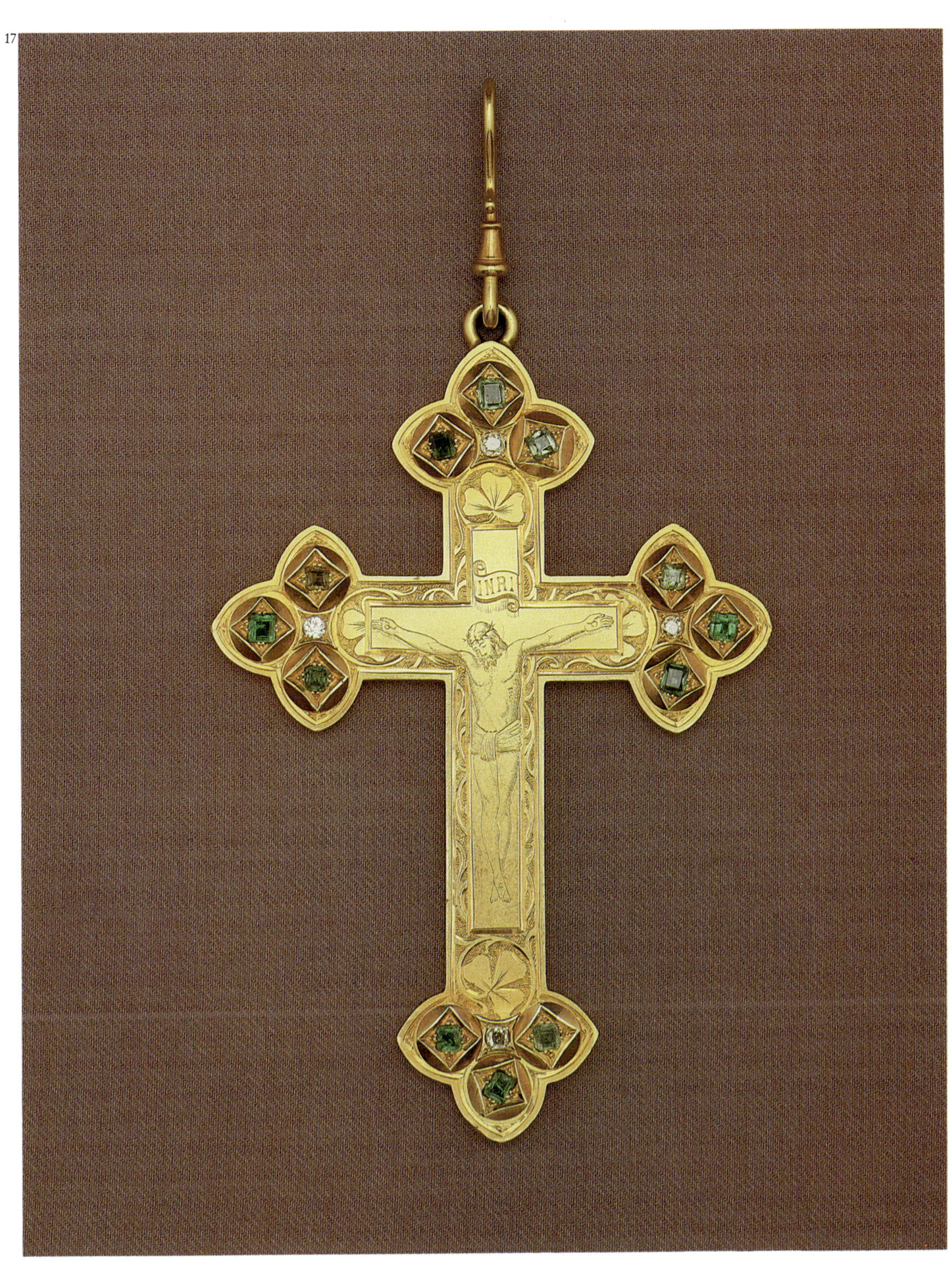

designer-maker and produced some very fine ecclesiastical work (see cat. 68). He also worked in collaboration with architects such as John Mockridge and Louis Williams (cat. 69) to produce schemes of decoration for new churches. Maurice Steeth died in 1970 and the business subsequently closed.

While the firms of F.J. Mole and W.J. Sanders have continued under new management, other large manufacturers of ecclesiastical wares such as Gaunt's, Pellegrini's and Steeth's ceased production during the course of the 1960s and 1970s. Nevertheless their legacy continues. Some of their workers have established their own metalworking businesses specializing in ecclesiastical wares. Terence County (cat. 99, 100) for example, trained at T. Gaunt & Co. (as did expatriate Stuart Devlin). When Albion (cat. 89), another important Melbourne firm, closed in 1979, its co-founder and manager Max Dewan went on to establish Dewan and Co. Pty. Ltd., while one of its silversmiths, René Hampl, opened his own business, Ecclesiastical Metalware (cat. 98). The existence of these and many other specialist workshops throughout the country demonstrates that the churches are still an important source of patronage for the Australian metalworking trade.

CRAFTWORKERS SINCE THE 1940s

Despite the dominant position of the larger trade workshops, independent craftworkers have continued to make a vital contribution to the furnishing of Australian churches since the second world war. The designs of the new generation of 'artist-craftsmen' exhibit a distinct stylistic break with the work of their predecessors. In the 1950s and 60s for example, the figurative metalwork designs of Dan Flynn, Emily Hope and Matcham Skipper fit comfortably within the stylistic ambience of contemporary Australian painting and sculpture. During the same period, the influence of modern Scandinavian and German design took hold in Australia, often directly transmitted by emigrant makers such as Helge Larsen and Ernest Fries.

From the late 1940s until his death in 1978, Victorian metalworker Dan Flynn produced some of the most original and technically ambitious work in the field.[35] A religious man, he devoted much of his time to ecclesiastical commissions, which could range from forging brass altar rails to fabricating a jewel-encrusted crown for a statue of the Virgin Mary (cat. 63).

The silver-gilt chalice of 1949 is his earliest work (cat 62). The figure of Christ crucified on a vine tree forms the stem, while the bowl rests within the outstretched arms. The strength of the piece derives not only from the fine modelling of the agonized figure but also from the successful combination of symbol and function. Christ nailed to the tree represents both the Tree of Life and the True Vine, summarizing the essence of the communion rite. Flynn's ability to translate symbol into object is exemplified again in the small but technically complex ciborium in enamel and silver-gilt (cat. 66). What more appropriate vessel for the communion wafers, the Body of Christ, than a fish, the symbol of Christ.

In an effort to invest his ecclesiastical work with cogent imagery, Flynn drew upon a variety of sources extending to the iconography of the Eastern Orthodox Church. In one of his most ambitious works, the tabernacle for St Mary's College, University of Melbourne (fig. 6), designed in conjunction with Mother Francis, the Superior of the college, the finely modelled images of the Madonna and saints were obviously inspired by Eastern icons. The central panel bears a representation of Rublev's *Christ Enthroned*, the Russian version of the Greek Pantocrator. Undoubtedly one of Flynn's best works, the tabernacle occupies a prominent position in the scheme of the chapel's decoration which includes woodwork by Schulim Krimper and sculpture by Andor Meszaros.

Emily Hope is another silversmith whose ecclesiastical work is rich in symbolic allusion. During the early 1960s, while still training as a gold and silversmith at the Royal Melbourne Institute of Technology, she became intensely interested in religion and began theology classes at Trinity College, University of Melbourne.[36] Her religious involvement found expression in a range of media—painting, sculpture and writing —but most definitely in her metalwork which was characteristically figurative and expressionistic.

In her ecclesiastical metalwork, Hope drew imaginatively upon biblical metaphor. The decoration of the chalice commissioned for St Anselm's,

35. Biographical information on Dan Flynn was generously provided by Mrs B. Flynn.
36. Rodriguez 1984, p.95.

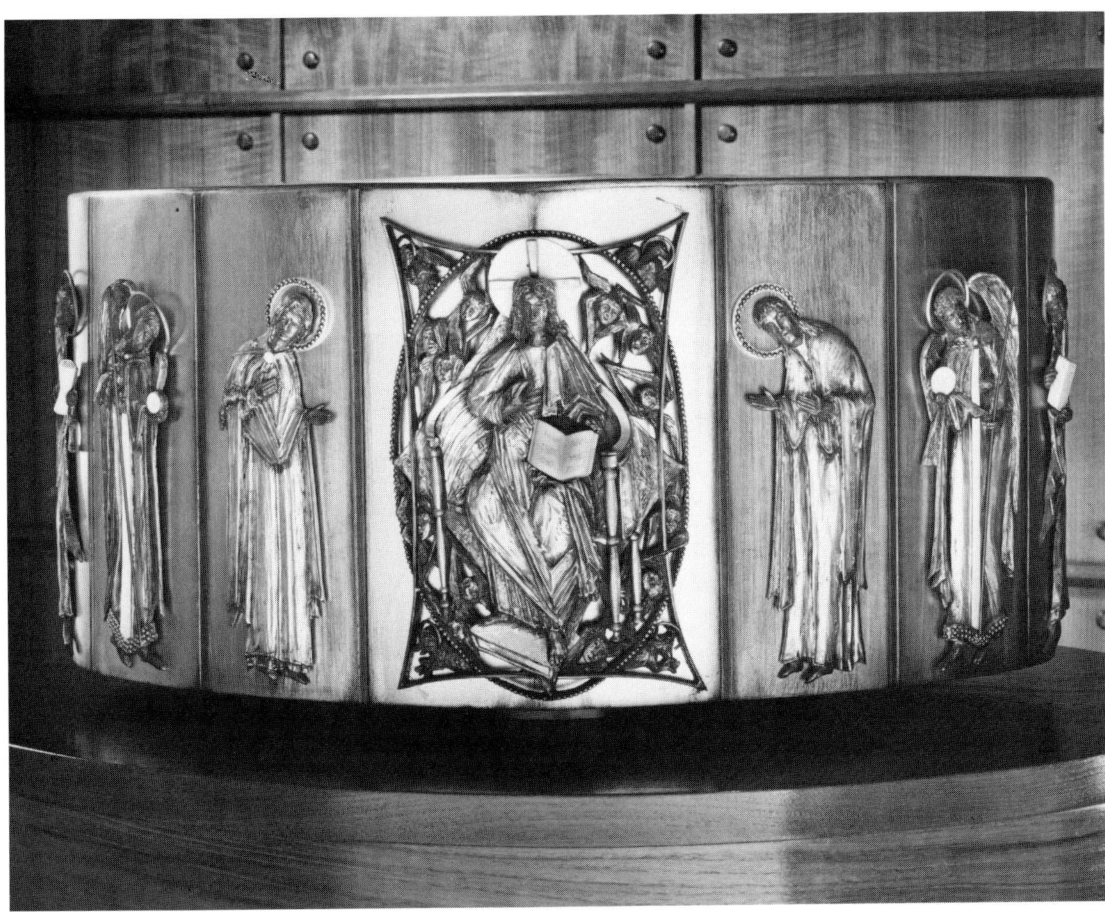

Middle Park (cat. 74) for example, was inspired by Revelations chapters 21 and 22. As described in the parish's *Church News*:

> On the foot of the chalice are four sapphires, bringing to mind the River of water of life, proceeding out of the throne of God (Verse 1). Growing from the River and cut in gilded silver is the Tree of Life, whose leaves in green enamel were for the healing of the nations (Verse 2) and from whose branches grow the 12 fruits and flowers which are represented by jewels—opals, emeralds, amethysts, diamonds, pearls, rubies, garnets, and topaz. Affixed to the Tree of Life is the figure of Christ in priestly vestments spread as on the Tree of the Cross offering the Sacrifice which gives the sacramental Life of God.[37]

Symbols of the four Evangelists frequently appear in Hope's work, for example on the chalice of 1962 (cat. 73) and in the pectoral cross of c.1970 (cat. 76). A group of lively cockatoos, which forms the stem of a small chalice (cat. 75), appears as a radical departure from the more traditional imagery. No doubt these birds are meant to be enjoyed as symbols of *joie de vivre*, but in this context they evoke the words of Psalm 148, 'Beasts, and all cattle; creeping things and flying fowl ... Praise ye the Lord'.

Unlike Emily Hope and Dan Flynn, Matcham Skipper does not claim a Christian commitment. Nonetheless he has undertaken a number of church commissions which have been successful by virtue of his evident understanding of the Christian subject matter. Primarily a jeweller, Skipper has

37. St Anselm's Church, *Church News* 21, 187, May 1964, pp.3–4.

45

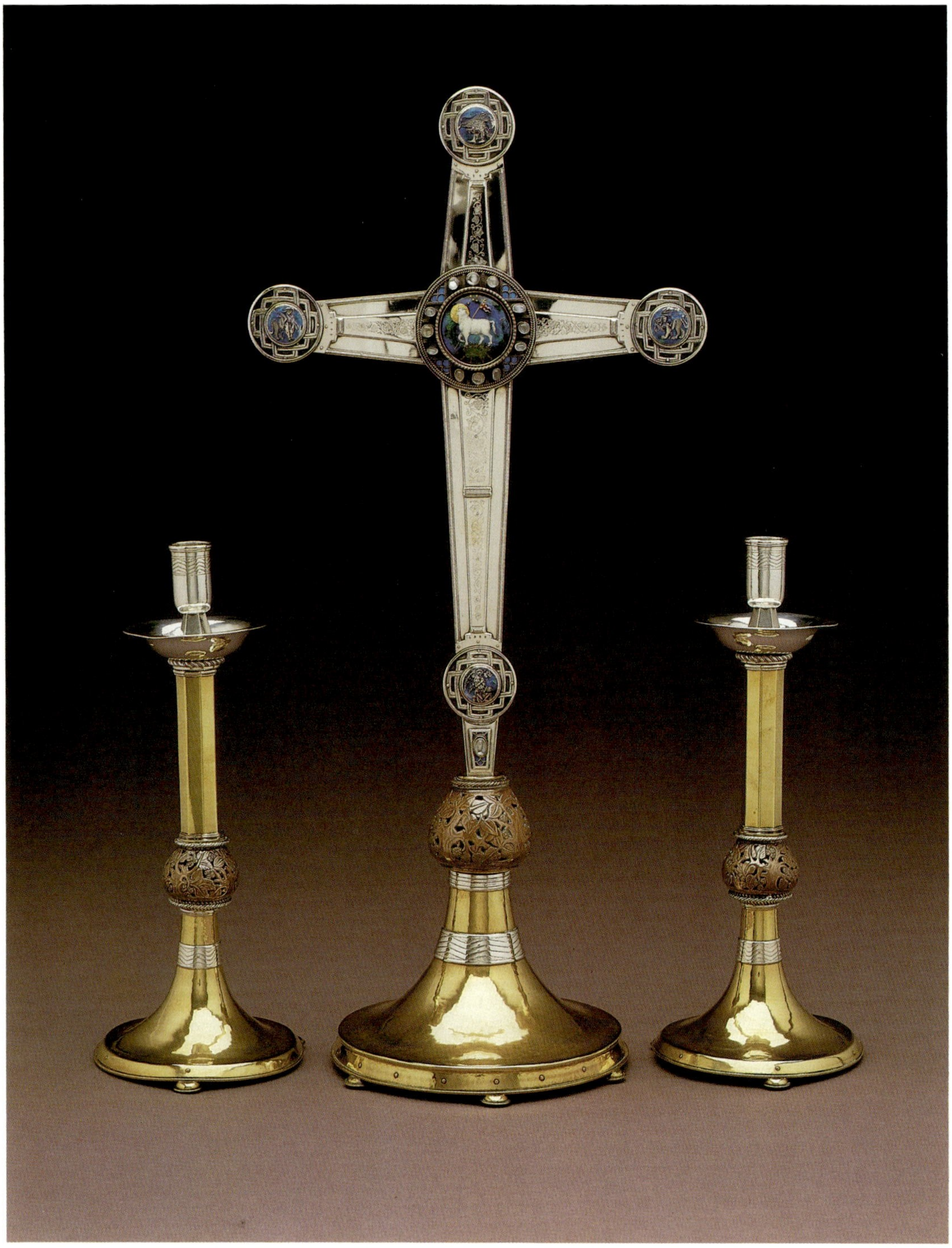

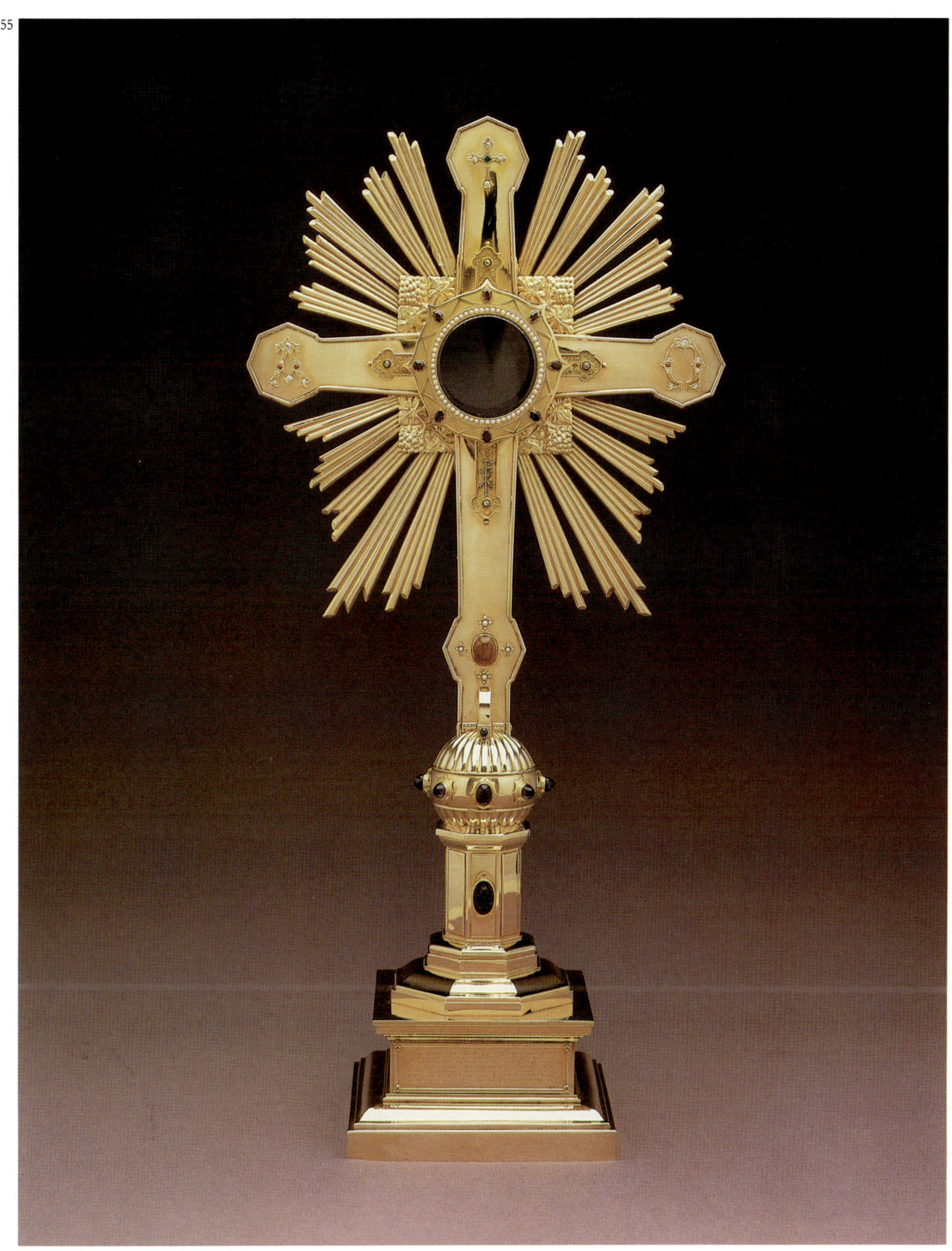

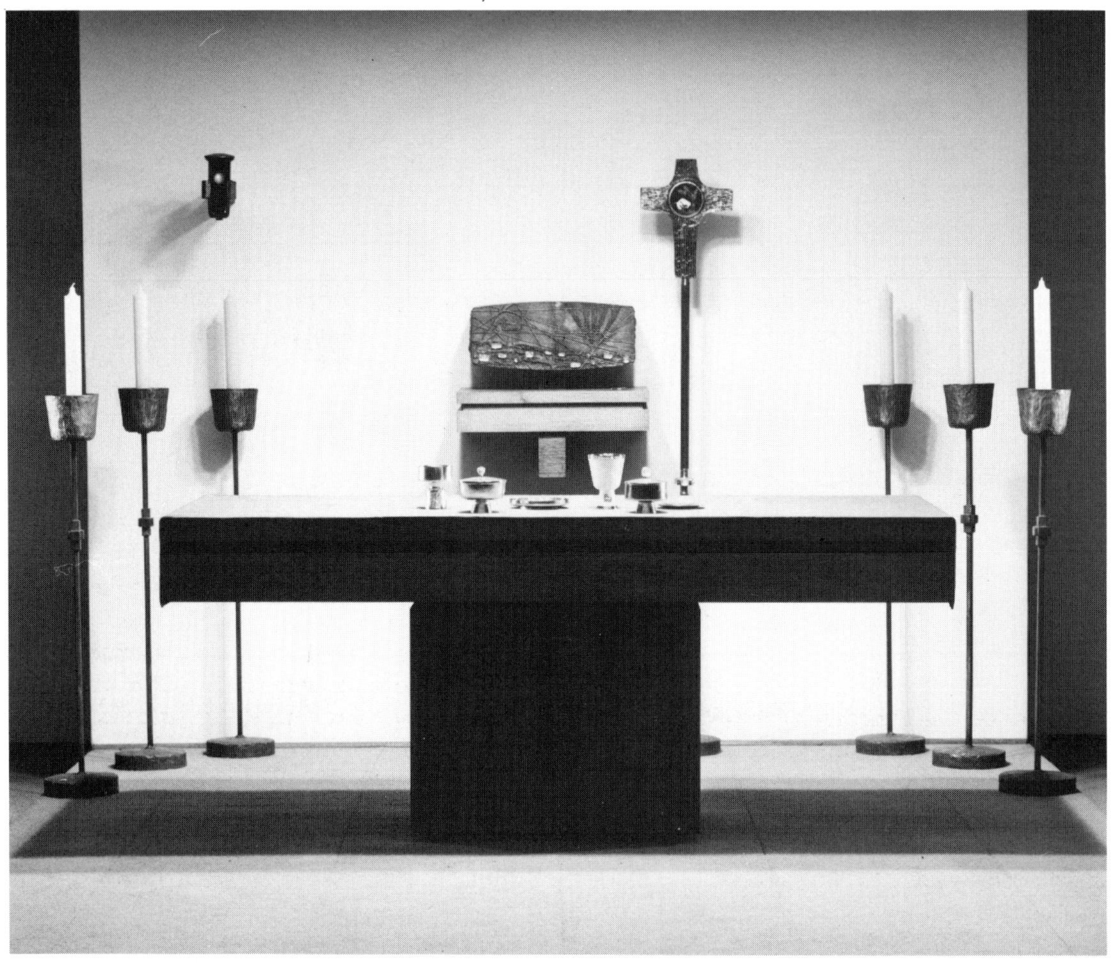

fig. 7
St Martin's in the Pines School Chapel, the metal furnishings
made by Ernest Fries c.1967

extended his metalsmithing to include sculptural commissions, the first of these being the Fourteen Stations of the Cross made for Mary Immaculate Catholic Church, Ivanhoe (cat. 72). The large cast panels, modelled variously in low and high relief, present a moving narrative of the Passion of Christ.

Sculptural commissions as such are not the subject of this exhibition, however a number of works by Australian sculptors have been included, being objects of a type more typically executed by metalsmiths. These are Hans Arkeveld's processional/altar cross (cat. 87) and Andor Meszaros' medallion series, the Fourteen Stations of the Cross (cat. 56).

The 1960s were prodigious for church building and associated craft commissions. Craftworkers were asked to make their contribution to the new and often radical concepts in church design and furnishing. Helge Larsen and Darani Lewers, for example, were invited by architects Clarke, Gazzard and Partners to produce six items of metalwork for the new Wentworth Memorial Church, Vaucluse in 1967 (cat. 86). Similarly, Perth architect Iris Rossen requested a number of artists and craftworkers, including Hans Arkeveld (cat. 87), David Walker and Geoffrey Allen, to make their individual contributions to the carefully orchestrated interior of St Dennis' Church, Joondanna. As a member of the Catholic Ecclesiastical Commission in Perth, Rossen has actively sought to make clergy and congregations aware of the advantages of utilizing local talent. In 1972 she helped to organize an exhibition of 'Religious and Liturgical Arts' in Perth, to which a number of Western Australian artists and craftworkers contributed, including Eric Carr (cat. 92–93) and Hans Arkeveld.

In some cases, a metalworker has been asked to provide most of the interior fittings of a church in sympathy with the architectural environment. Silversmith/sculptor Ernest Fries has provided a number of such settings, a fine example being St Martin's in the Pines School Chapel (fig. 7). A singular translation of architectural concept into object may be observed in the communion service (cat. 90) made by Robert Baines for All Saints' Church, Greensborough. Baines employed the unusual diamond-shaped floor plan and the pyramidal ceiling of the church as the formal reference for his designs. Each of the three pieces of holloware has this geometry in common, especially the bread box which is like a miniature version of the church. The inset panels of blue, yellow and purple enamel refer to the stained glass windows of the building.

Whereas commissions such as this may be inspired by the formal qualities of the architecture, other liturgical pieces have been designed in response to the particular situation of the patron. The form of the chalice and paten made by Ernest Fries for the first Aboriginal Catholic priest (cat. 85), for example, derives from the long wooden carrying dishes (generally known as coolamons) used by Australian Aborigines. Both pieces were carved in wood; the chalice was given a silver-gilt lining to signify its special sacred function, while a thin line of silver was used to highlight the rim of the paten.

A chalice and paten by John and Dan Flynn (cat. 97), sons of the late Dan Flynn, were also commissioned under special circumstances. In 1983, the Church of the Good Shepherd, Mt Macedon was destroyed in the Ash Wednesday bushfires. The chalice belonging to the church, or at least what was left of its bowl, was salvaged from the ruins. In the process of planning a new church, the parish decided to commission a replacement chalice, but one which would incorporate the remnant of the original. The Flynns responded by making a plain ebony and silver stem, half formed as a cross, to support the old bowl. While gilding the interior of the latter, they retained the rough exterior surface which had been blackened by the fire. A clear and simple statement, it not only embodies a tangible element of the parish's history but also expresses its implicit faith in the future.

The ecclesiastical commission remains one of the few forms of patronage which allows the craftworker to create an object of greater significance than its own intrinsic value or marketability. A vital tradition can be maintained if the churches continue to provide Australian metalsmiths with the opportunity to work within this stimulating context.

63

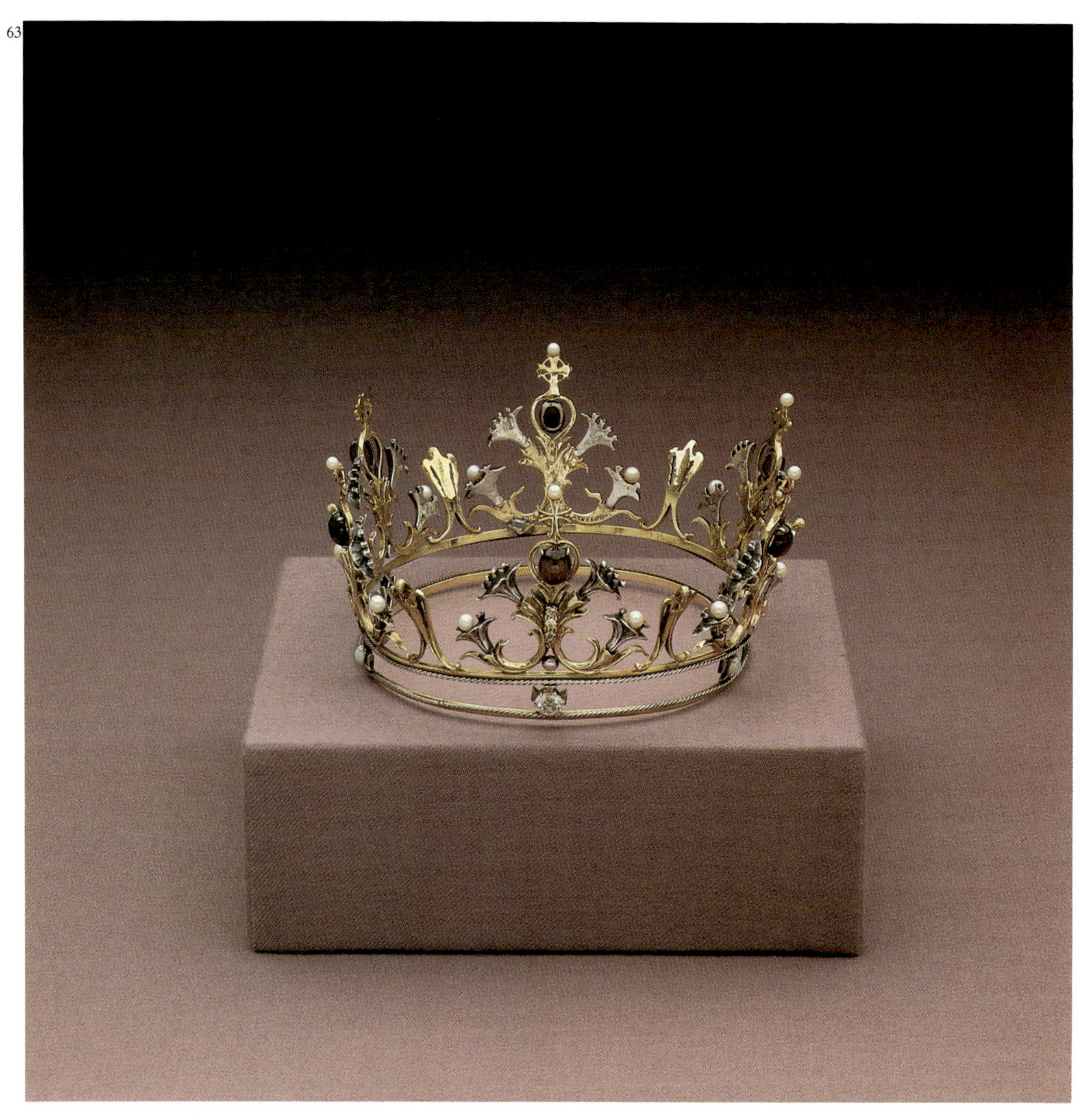

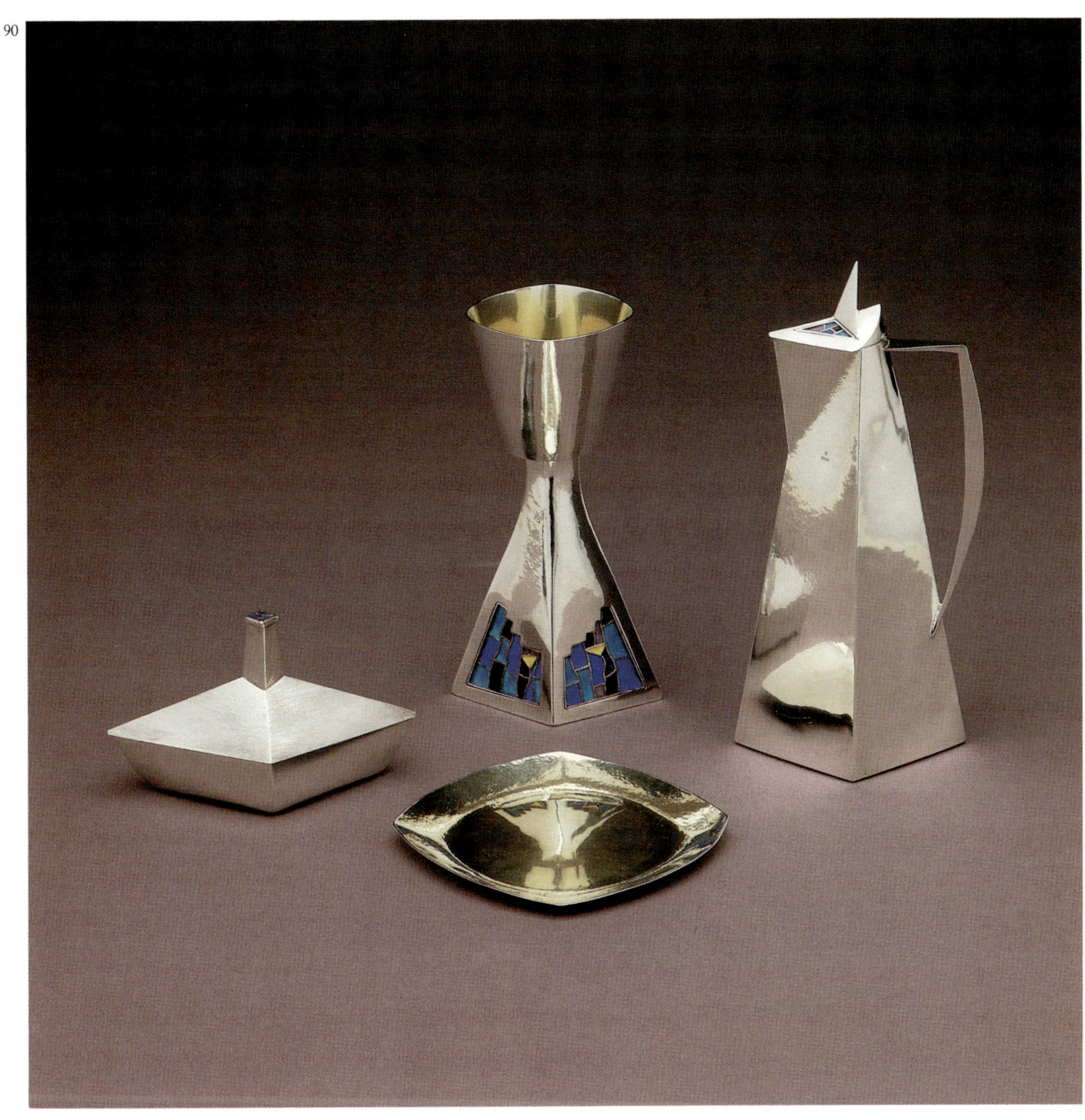

James Robertson—Sydney

B.Scotland 1781 arr.1822 d.1868

1. CHALICE, one of pair
1826
Silver
H.18 d.11.8
Inscribed: 'Presented to the Scots Church, Sydney By
JOHN DUNMORE LANG D.D. Minister 1826'
Scots Church, Sydney
Literature: Hawkins 1973, p.15, item 5, illus.
Hawkins states that the chalices are likely to have
been made by Alexander Dick who worked for
Robertson from 1824–26.

The campana-shaped bowl, the lower part with vertical lobed fluting, rests on a convex stem which expands to a stepped circular foot, is annulated at the
waist and has a projecting collar.

Charles Firnhaber—Adelaide

B.Germany 1806 arr.1847 d.1880

2. COMMUNION SERVICE—CHALICE, PATEN,
EWER
c.1856
Silver, silver-gilt
Chalice h.24.2 d.12.8
Paten w.23.4
Ewer h.32
The Anglican Parish of Mt Barker,
South Australia
Note: Made for The Anglican Church of St James,
Blakiston, South Australia
Literature: The Adelaide Times, 22 January 1856

The bowl of the chalice, with everted lip, has its
lower part lobed and embossed with flowers and
foliage. The tapering stem, low set knop and foot,
with moulded circular base, are lobed and ribbed.
The upper part of the stem and the rim of the foot
are embossed with flowers and foliage.

The sexfoil paten is applied with fruiting vine
motif at the rim. Its deep central depression has an
applied IHS ('H' missing) over cross, over radiating
twelve point star in silver-gilt.

The flagon has a spouted pear-shaped body with
applied IHS over cross, over radiating twelve point
star in silver-gilt and rests on a domed foot embossed
with a band of flowers and foliage. The domed cover
is similarly decorated and has a high thumbrest
which is attached to a double scroll handle.

William Edwards—Melbourne

Active c.1860–73
Edwards and Kaul c.1874–92

3. PAIR OF CHALICES AND PATENS
c.1866
Silver-gilt
Chalice h.26.5 w.17
Paten d.15.6
Inscribed: On one chalice 'Presented by The Right
Revd. Dr. Shiel, Bishop of Adelaide to The Very

Rev'd. Dr. Fitzpatrick V.G. Melbourne Septr. 1866'
St Patrick's Catholic Cathedral, Melbourne
Note: The chalices bear both William Edwards' mark
and the retail mark of Walsh Brothers of Melbourne.

Each bowl has a calyx of openwork tracery with leaf
motifs. The hexagonal stem is decorated with a
repeated Gothic fenestration motif and has a
compressed spherical knop with six lozenge-shaped
bosses. The hexagonal foot on sexfoil base is
embellished with traceried and leaf motifs and a
cross.

The circular paten is engraved with an *Agnus Dei*
encircled by a crown of thorns.

Christian Ludwig Qwist—Sydney

B. Denmark 1818 arr.1852 d.1877

4. CHALICE, one of a pair
c.1868
Silver
H.22.7 w.11.5
Congregational Church, Pitt Street, Sydney
Literature: Hawkins 1973, pp.32–3, item 31, illus.

The lobed bowl, with everted lip, rests on a convex
fluted stem with a double annular knop. The lobed
foot has a circular base of eight lobes.

Denis Brothers—Melbourne
c.1853–1910

5. CHALICE
c.1870
Silver-gilt
H.26.6 d.14.5
Catholic Diocese of Melbourne

The bowl, with everted lip, rests on a baluster stem;
the domical foot has a moulded circular base.

6. CHALICE
c.1870
Silver
H.23
Private collection, Sydney
Literature: Hawkins 1973, p.110, item 168, illus.

The bowl has a calyx of openwork floral and leaf
motifs. The stem, knop and foot are hexagonal. The
vertical edge of the sexfoil base has a pierced band of
quatrefoil pattern. Fruiting vine and pendant leaf
motifs are applied to the knop and foot.

7. CHALICE AND PATEN
1885
Gold, precious stones
Chalice h.27.5 d.15.2
Paten d.13.8
Inscribed: 'ME SACERDOTES SANDHURSTENSIS
STEPHANO REVILLE EPISCOPODIE
CONSECRATIONIS EJUS DONARUNT MART
II XXIX MDCCCLXXXV'
Sacred Heart Catholic Cathedral, Bendigo, Victoria

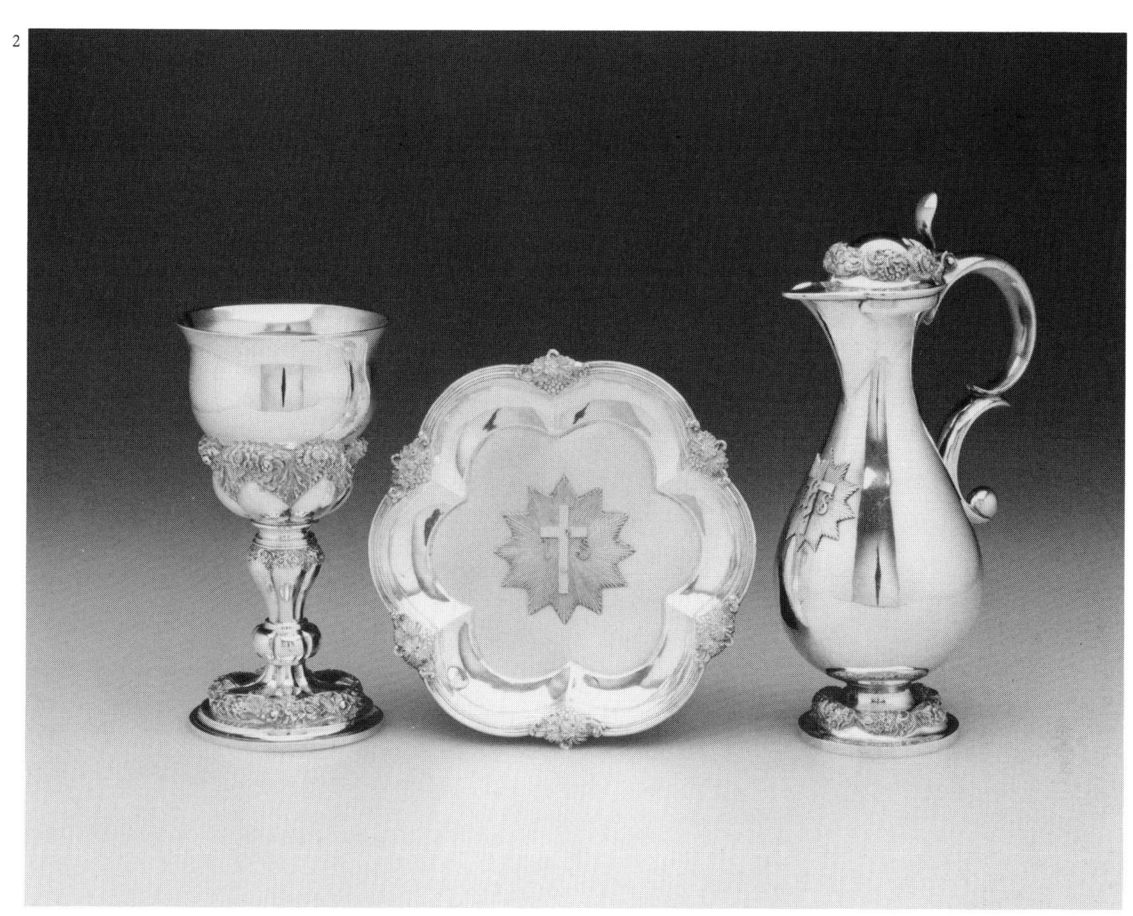

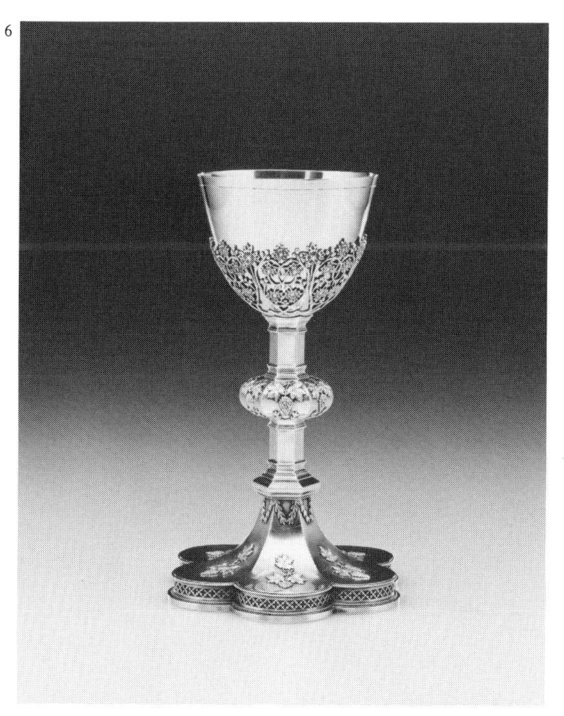

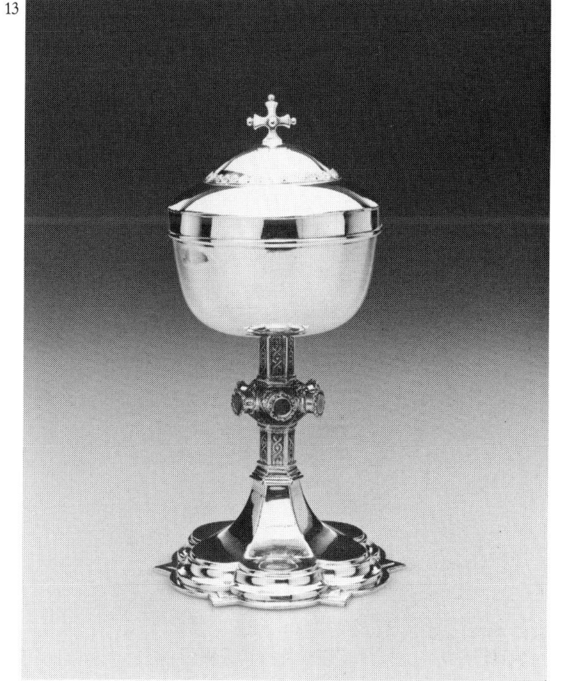

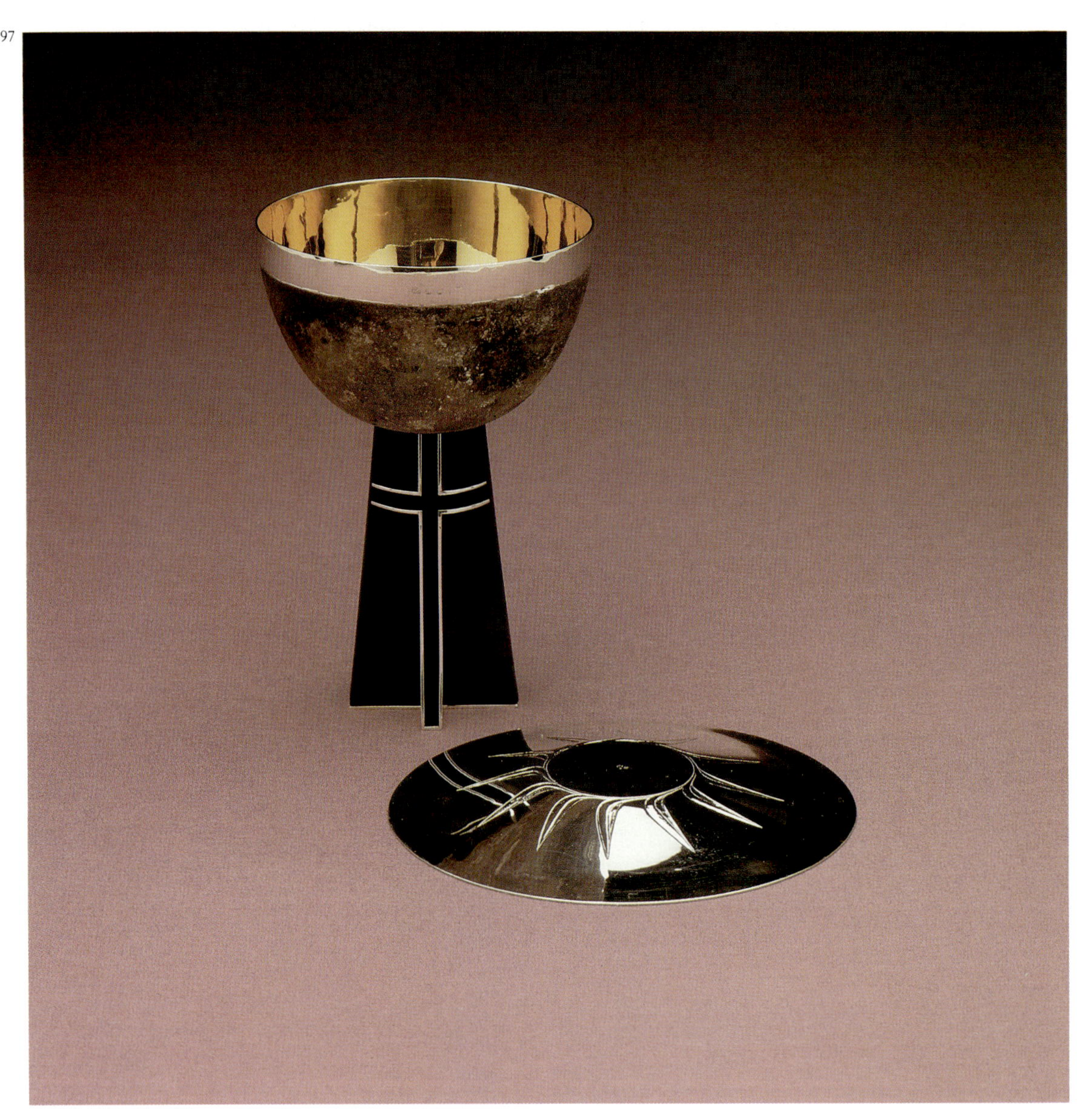

The bowl is engraved with IHS over cross within rays and applied with repeated stylized leaf and flower motifs around the lower part. The baluster stem is elaborately chased and engraved and set with stones. The moulded knop, with applied 'SR' monogram on a shield, is set with eight stones including four within deep hexagonal bezels. The domed foot, with applied cross patée, has a moulded circular base with two bands of chased and engraved decoration.

The circular paten is engraved with IHS over cross within rays.

8. CHALICE AND PATEN
c.1890
Silver, silver-gilt
Chalice h.24.5 w.12.1
Paten d.12.8
Inscribed: 'Loretto Convent, Albert Park'
St Mary's College, University of Melbourne

The bowl is encircled by an engraved band of festoons. The annulated stem has a circular knop with an indented annular projection. The high hexagonal foot, on sexfoil base, is engraved with leaf and shamrock motifs and applied with a mandola containing a cross.

The circular paten is engraved with a cross, with fleur-de-lis terminals, over a quatrefoil.

Hippolyte Delarue—Sydney
B.France c.1829 arr.1850 d.1881

9. PECTORAL CROSS
c.1870
Gold, silver, rubies, containing relics of SS Peter and John
L.13.3 w.9.3
St Mary's Catholic Cathedral, Sydney

The cross is elaborately engraved with scrolling, geometric and shamrock motifs. Each of the four arms is set with a stone. At the intersection of the arms is an applied silver lamb on an engraved gold roundel with four stones set at its rim. The reverse has a hinged reliquary at the intersection of the arms.

Henry Steiner—Adelaide
B.Germany 1835 arr.1858 d.Germany 1914

10. CHALICE
c.1875
Silver-gilt
H.21.8 d.12.9
Lent by J. Klinger Esq., Adelaide
Literature: Hawkins 1973, p.69, item 81

The lower part of the bowl is engraved to delineate a calyx. The cylindrical stem has a compressed spherical knop. The trumpet foot, on circular base, is engraved with a band of scalloped decoration and a cross patée convex.

E.J. Hollingdale—Sydney
B.1832 d.1882
E.J. Hollingdale & Son c.1882–97
(E.J.) Hollingdale & Kessel c.1898–1934

11. CROZIER
1877
Gold, myall wood
H.180.5
St Mary's Catholic Cathedral, Sydney
Note: Presented to The Most Reverend Roger Vaughan, Archbishop of Sydney in 1877
Literature: Sydney Mail, 3 March 1877, pp.4–5, illus. Town and Country Journal (NSW), 3 March 1877, p.344, illus.
Hawkins 1973, pp.44–5, item 45, illus.

The gold head is of scrolling foliate design. The myall wood shaft is in three parts; the junctures and tip have applied leaf borders in gold.

12. PECTORAL CROSS
1919
Gold
L.12.3 w.8.3
Inscribed: 'W. BARRY SYDNEY 31.9.1919'
St Mary's Catholic Cathedral, Hobart

The arms of the cross, which terminate in trefoils, are engraved with scrolling and foliate motifs and the intersection of the obverse is engraved with an IHS monogram.

John McLean & Son—Sydney
c.1874–96

13. CIBORIUM, one of pair
c.1879
Electroplate
H.28.5 w.16.1
St Mary's Catholic Cathedral, Sydney
Literature: Hawkins 1973, pp.46–47, item 46, illus.

The bowl rests on a hexagonal stem chased with an interlaced pattern. The chased knop has six circular bosses, each face is decorated with stylized floral motif and encircled by a fine chain. The hexagonal foot has a stepped sexfoil base. The cover, in the form of a stepped dome, has an applied band of repeated leaf motif and is surmounted by a cross finial with bead terminals.

Edward Francis Gunter Fischer—Geelong and Melbourne
B.Austria 1828 arr.1851 d.1911

14. CIBORIUM
Last quarter 19th century
Silver, silver-gilt
H.25 d.10.3
National Gallery of Victoria
The J. and J. Altmann Collection of Australian Silver:presented through The Art Foundation of Victoria 1979
D223/1979

Literature: The J. and J. Altmann Collection of Australian Silver, Exhibition catalogue, National Gallery of Victoria, Melbourne, 1981, item 64

The bowl rests on a cylindrical stem chased with two bands of repeated leaf motif. The compressed spherical knop has two bands of leaf motif forming a band of six lozenges at their juncture. The domed foot, on circular base, is embossed with wheat, fruiting vine and scrolling foliate motifs. The cover is embossed with fruiting vine and wheat motifs and surmounted by a cross in silver-gilt.

Frederick Basse—Adelaide
Active c.1880–1910

15. TRAVELLING COMMUNION SERVICE
c.1890
Silver, glass, wood, leather, plush
Box h.7.3 w.12
National Gallery of Victoria.
Presented by Kozminsky Galleries 1978
D45/1978

The bowl of the chalice has an everted lip and is engraved with an IHS within an eight pointed star. The stem flares into a trumpet foot on circular base.

The circular paten has a central depression engraved with an eight pointed star.

The glass wine bottle, with cork stopper, has a painted floral motif on both obverse and reverse.

The service retains its original fitted box.

J.T. Sleep—Melbourne
Active c.1884–95

16. CHALICE
1893
Gold
H.22 w.11.6
Inscribed: 'This Chalice of Ballarat Gold presented to The Most Reverend Dr. Delany D.D. Bishop of Laranda and Coadjutor Bishop of Hobart by Ballarat friends in commemoration of his Consecration at St. Patricks's Cathedral Ballarat on the 10th December 1893'
St Mary's Catholic Cathedral, Hobart

The bowl is engraved with a band of scrolling foliate decoration and an IHS monogram within a shield. The cylindrical stem and compressed spherical knop are annulated. The domed foot, engraved with a band of scrolling foliate decoration, is set on a circular base.

T.Gaunt & Co.—Melbourne
c.1856–1979

17. PECTORAL CROSS
Possibly designed by William Wardell
c.1897
Gold, diamonds, emeralds
L.17 w.9.3

St Patrick's Catholic Cathedral, Melbourne
Literature: The Advocate, 30 October 1897, p.16

The arms of the cross terminate in trefoils, each set with four stones. The surface is engraved with the figure of Christ crucified and two shamrocks. Wheat and a fruiting vine are engraved on the reverse.

18. MONSTRANCE
c.1897
Silver-gilt, paste
H.77.2 w.38
St Patrick's Catholic Cathedral, Melbourne
Literature: The Advocate, 30 October 1897, p.16

The glazed roundel for the Host is encircled by a band of trefoil pattern set with stones. From this extends a border of stamped fruiting vine motif divided by four wheat motifs, and behind this extend wavy rays. The hexagonal stem, compressed spherical knop and hexagonal foot, on moulded sexfoil base, are elaborately chased with wheat, leaf, and fruiting vine motifs. The whole is surmounted by a cross.

19. CHALICE
c.1897
Gold
H.23.4 d.12.7
St Patrick's Catholic Cathedral, Melbourne

The bowl rests on a cylindrical stem with a chased, compressed, spherical knop. The trumpet foot, on circular base, has rays emerging below the annular junction with stem and is embellished with leaf and wheat motifs and applied with a cross in gold.

20. PECTORAL CROSS
c.1900
Gold, diamonds, emeralds, containing relic of the Holy Cross
L.12.2 w.9.2
Sacred Heart Catholic Cathedral, Bendigo, Victoria

The arms of the cross, terminating in fleur-de-lis stemming from a bulb of flat section, are set with fourteen stones. A large rectangular stone is set at the intersection within an applied flat roundel. The reverse is engraved with a cross patée convex and geometric motifs.

21. CHALICE
1916
Gold, enamel
H.22.5 w.14.6
Inscribed: 'Presented to the Very Rev Fr. Daniel Foley on his appointment as Bishop of Ballarat by his Parishioners Terang Parish Aug. 15th. 1916'
Catholic Diocese of Ballarat, Victoria

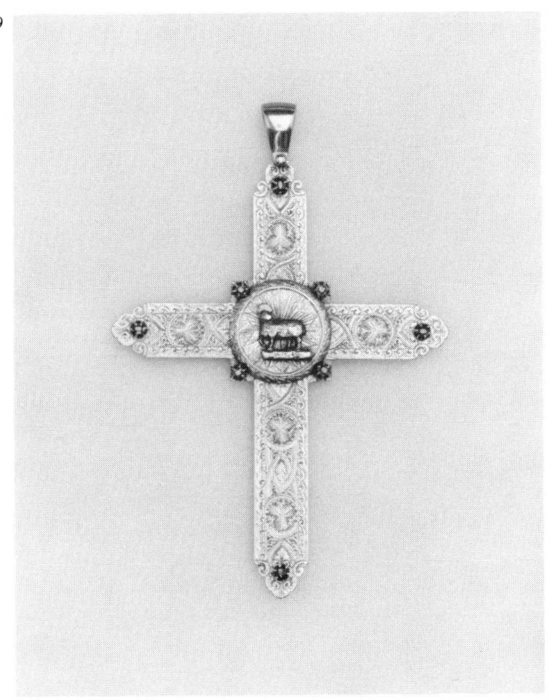 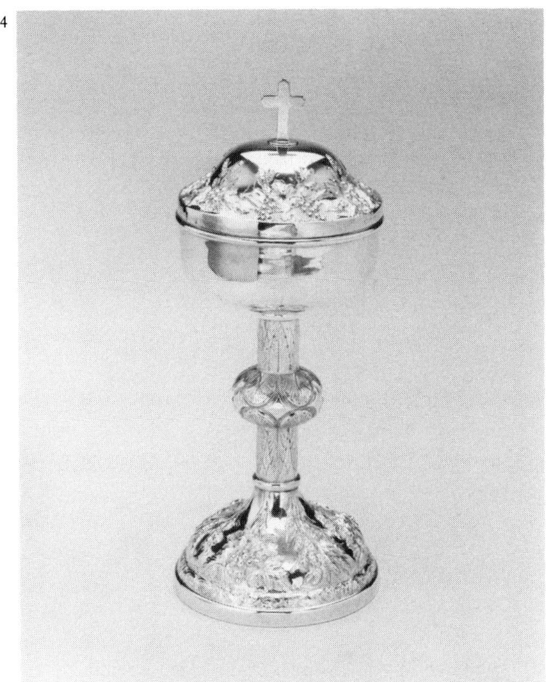

The bowl has an engraved calyx. The cylindrical
stem has a compressed spherical knop with engraved decoration and a central band of applied stylized
flowers. The quatrefoil foot is engraved with
fruiting vine and scrolling motifs and has an applied
enamelled cross. The quatrefoil base has four scrolling buttresses attached to the foot.

22. CROZIER
1930
Silver-gilt
H.191
Inscribed: 'PRESENTED TO THE RIGHT REV.
JAMES P. O'COLLINS BISHOP OF
GERALDTON by the MEMBERS of the
MANLY UNION. May 11th 1930'
Catholic Diocese of Ballarat, Victoria

The outer surface of the head is crocketed, its
inward curve terminating in an encircled cross. The
annulated capital of the shaft has a square knop,
with four quatrefoils engraved with devotional
images, below which is a compressed spherical
knop with four applied mandolas, each engraved
with a flower motif. The silver-gilt shaft, in three
parts, has one square and two spherical knops and
is decorated at the junctures with applied bands of
repeated leaf motif.

23. CHALICE AND PATEN
1941
Gold, precious and semi-precious stones
Chalice h.21.1 d.16.5
Paten d.16.8

Inscribed: 'CENTENARY OF ST. FRANCIS'
CHURCH 4TH OCT. 1841 4TH OCT. 1941
GIFT OF BENEFACTORS AND FRIENDS'
Catholic Diocese of Melbourne
Note: The chalice and paten were made from
donated gold and jewellery.
Literature: Rogan 1976, p.11, cat.97

The bowl of the chalice is set with stones and is
elaborately embossed with scrolling foliate motifs
which form six cartouches engraved with
devotional images. The chased knop has a central
band set with stones. The trumpet foot, embossed
with scrolling foliate motifs, has six applied panels
of gold set with stones, between which are five
engraved scenes depicting features of St Francis'
Church and an applied encircled cross set with
stones.

The circular paten is engraved with a cross patée
convex incorporating five symbolic images, which is
encircled by an engraved band of scrolling foliate
decoration and an applied beaded wire.

24. BISHOP'S RING
c.1947
Gold, silver, sapphire, diamonds
H.3.3
Sacred Heart Catholic Cathedral, Bendigo, Victoria

The gold ring is set with a faceted sapphire surrounded by diamonds. Each shoulder is applied
with a silver cross patée with an embossed central
roundel, one depicting the head of Christ, the
other the head of the Madonna.

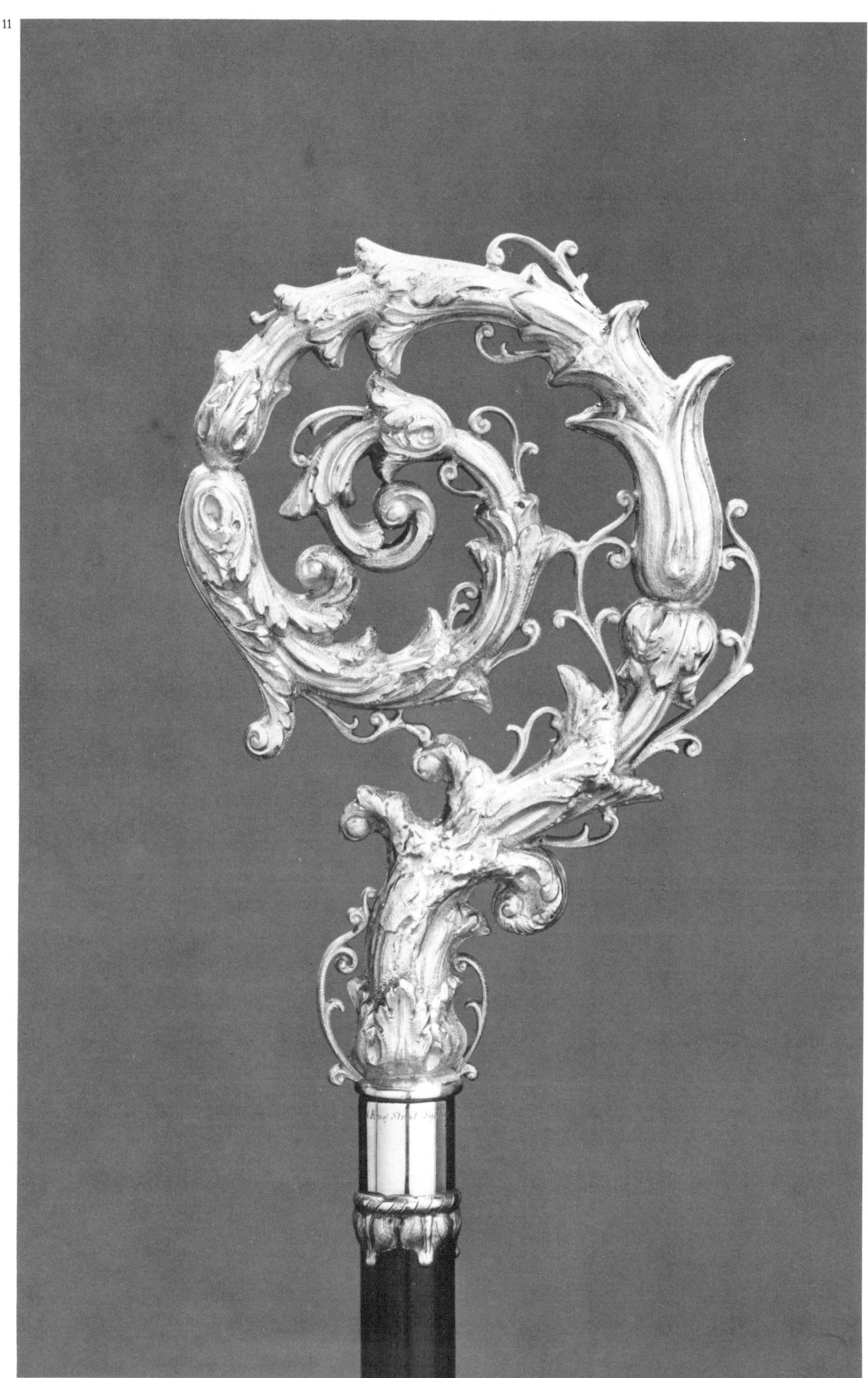

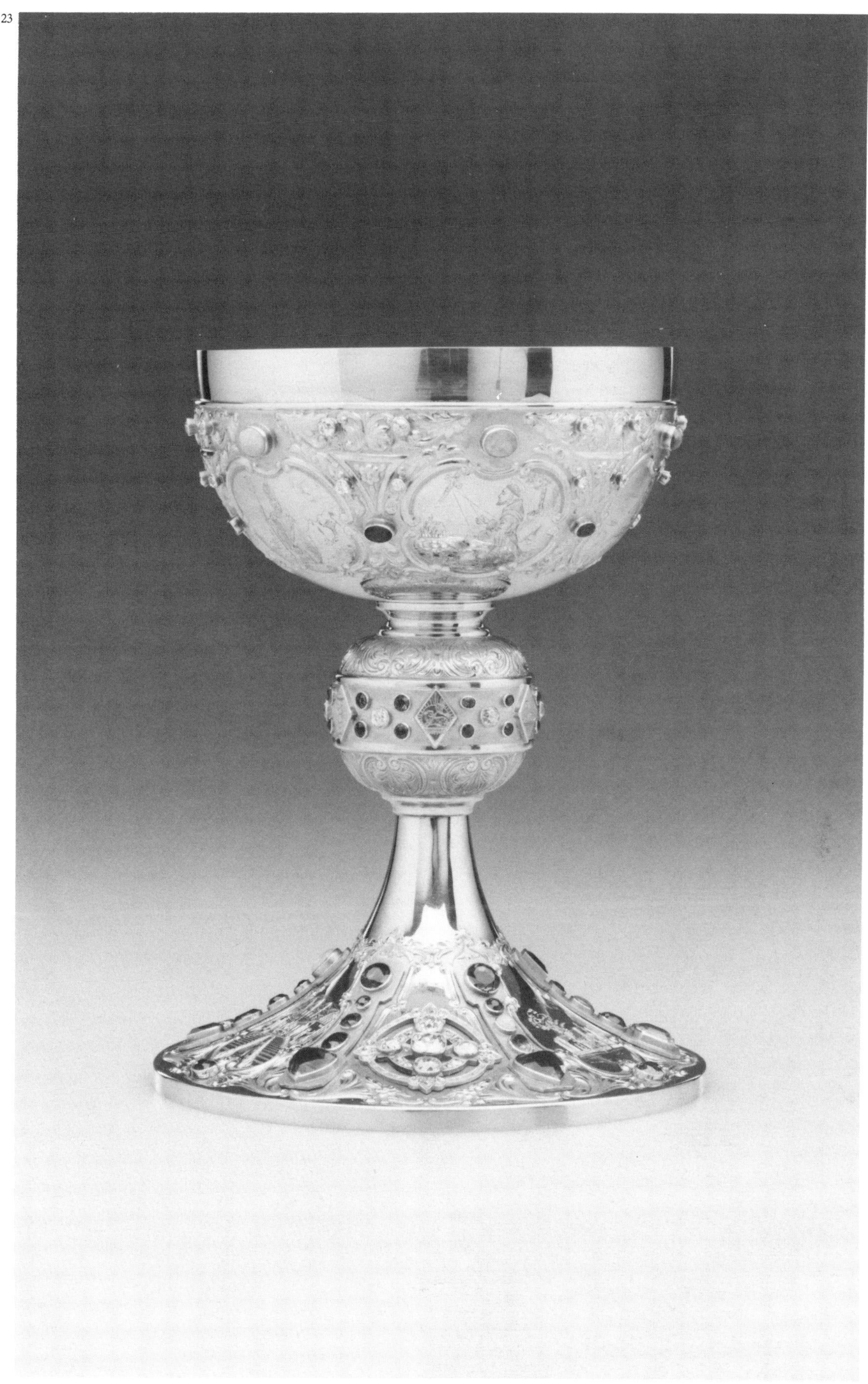

Harry Trantum—Kalgoorlie, Western
Australia
Active c.1890–1923

25. PECTORAL CROSS
1903
Gold, tourmaline
L.10.3 w.6.7
Inscribed: (At a later date) 'Presented by The
CHRISTIAN BROTHERS To THE MOST REV.
J.B. ROPER D.D. BISHOP OF TOOWOOMBA
28.9.38'
Catholic Diocesan Archives, Toowoomba,
Queensland
Note: Presented to The Most Reverend Matthew
Gibney D.D. by the parishioners of Kalgoorlie in
1903
Literature: The Leader, 23 September 1979; article
by Br. L.J. Ansell, C.F.C.

The celtic cross is set with a faceted tourmaline at
the intersection of its arms and is decorated with
applied trailing shamrocks, four celtic crosses, and
engraved leafy sprays. The reverse is engraved with
scrolling foliate decoration and a gold cross is
applied at the intersection of the arms.

J.W.R. Linton—Perth
B.England 1869 arr.1896 d.1947
Partnership with Arthur Cross c.1910–17

26. CHALICE
c.1910
Silver, gold, garnets
H.21.9 w.12
Lent by John Linton Esq., Perth

The bowl has a scalloped calyx incorporating fleur-
de-lis motifs. Four bands of plaited wire are applied
to the hexagonal stem. The compressed spherical
knop has four lozenge-shaped bosses set with
cabochon garnets and is inset with a band of wavy
wire. The hexagonal foot, on sexfoil base, is set
with six cabochon garnets.

27. ALTAR CROSS AND CANDLESTICKS
c.1932
Brass, enamel
Cross h.69 w.26
Candlesticks h.49 w.55.5
Inscribed: 'To the Glory of God and in Loving
Memory of GERTRUDE MABEL MAY
EDWARDS 25 years a faithful ''G.F.S''
Worker'

The Anglican Parish of Christ Church, Claremont,
Western Australia
Note: Drawing lent by the Western Australian
Museum

A leaf and strapwork motif is applied to each of the
upper arms of the cross. The intersection of the
arms is set with a circular enamel depicting a cross,
while the junctures are inset with openwork scrolling wire. The domed base, set on four scroll feet, is
applied with a scrolling motif and stylized flowers.

Each candlestick has a tapering cylindrical stem
which is applied with decorated bands at the
juncture with the conical drip pan and with the
base. The domed base, set on four scroll feet, is
applied with scrolling motif and stylized flowers.

Attributed to J.W.R. Linton

28. CHALICE
1911
Silver, garnets
H.22.8 d.11.1
Inscribed: 'ST. GEORGE'S CATHEDRAL,
PERTH, W.A. A HUMBLE THANK
OFFERING TO ALMIGHTY GOD FROM
HENRY GUY DAMPIER LATHAM, (DEAN
OF THIS CATHEDRAL, 1906–1911) AND
FLORENCE GERTRUDE, HIS WIFE.
WHITSUNTIDE, 1911'
St George's Anglican Cathedral, Perth

The bowl rests on a cylindrical stem embossed with
diagonal convex fluting. The knop expands into
four lozenge-shaped bosses, each set with a
cabochon garnet. The trumpet foot has a circular
base.

Kuster—Melbourne
Active c.1911–17

29. FONT EWER
1912
Brass, copper, enamel, wood
H.38 w.28
Inscribed: 'This FONT EWER Presented to All
Saints Church Geelong, By THE G.F.S.
CANDIDATES CHRISTMAS 1912'
All Saints' Anglican Church, Geelong, Victoria

The spouted cylindrical body, with a low set
horizontal handle and band of embossed gum
leaves, rests on a domed base. A cross in copper and
black enamel is applied to the front of the body. A
bail handle, with wooden hand-grip, is attached to
the body just below the rim. The cover is shaped
to accommodate the spout and has an applied
handle.

James McBean & Son—Melbourne
c.1858–1927

30. SET OF OIL STOCKS
1916
Silver-gilt, semi-precious stones
H.12 w.7
Inscribed: On each 'Daniel Mannix Archiepus Dono
dedit Danieli Foley Episcopo Ballaraten'
Catholic Diocese of Ballarat, Victoria

The three oil stocks are of identical design. The
thistle-shaped bowl, embossed with a repeated leaf
motif around the lower part, rests on a low
trumpet foot on a stepped circular base. The low-
domed cover is embossed with the same repeated
leaf motif and is surmounted by a cross patée
convex finial. Each rim is set with four stones in

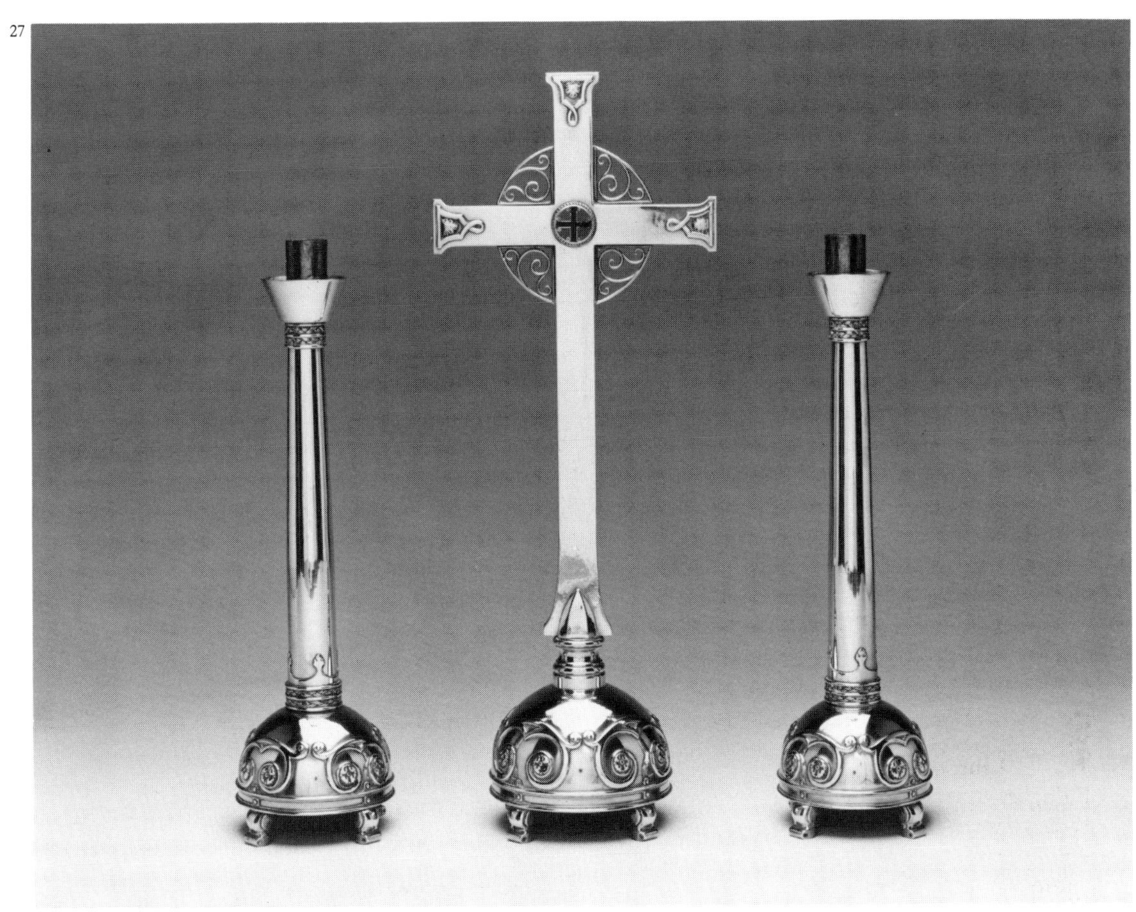

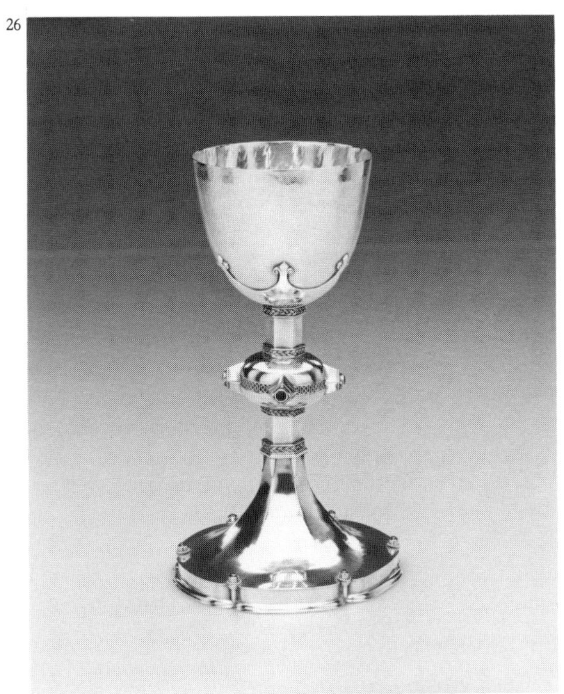

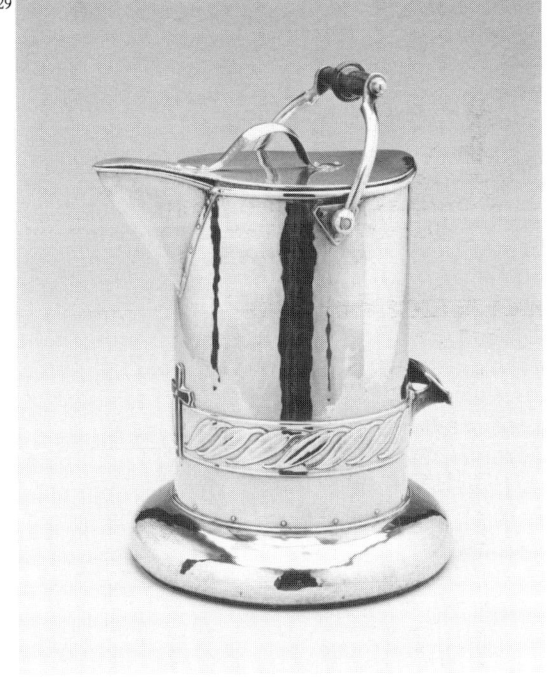

square bezels and bears an engraved inscription to designate the stock's intended use, reading separately as follows: 'C.A.T. Die 24 Aug 1916' 'I.N.F. Die 24 Aug 1916' and 'C.H.R. Die 24 Aug 1916'.

F.J. Mole (now F.J. Mole & Co.)—Brisbane
Established 1913

31. CHALICE AND PATEN
1918
Silver, silver-gilt, gold, precious stones
Chalice h.22 w.14.8
Paten d.14.6
Inscribed: 'Presented to REV. O.S. HAYES on his
ordination 30th NOV. 1918'
Pius XII Provincial Seminary, Banyo, Queensland

The bowl has a calyx of openwork tracery. The
hexagonal stem has twelve panels of partially
pierced Gothic fenestration. The compressed
spherical knop, with pierced traceried motifs, has
six lozenge-shaped bosses, together spelling 'INS
IHS'. The hexagonal foot has Gothic arches applied
below the juncture with stem and is applied with a
gold cross set with stones. The vertical edge of the
sexfoil base has a band of open quatrefoil pattern.
The paten is flat and circular.

32. CIBORIUM
c.1922
Silver, silver-gilt, precious and semi-precious
stones, pearls
H.30.5 w.14.6
Inscribed: 'IN MEMORY OF ALICE MARY
GENEVIEVE HAYES DIED, SANDGATE Q.
MAY 3RD 1922'
Pius XII Provincial Seminary, Banyo, Queensland

The bowl has a calyx of openwork tracery. The
hexagonal stem is decorated with a repeated Gothic
fenestration motif. The compressed spherical knop
has six lozenge-shaped bosses set with stones
within six oval bezels. The hexagonal foot has
Gothic arches applied below the juncture with
stem. The vertical edge of the sexfoil base has a
band of open quatrefoil pattern. The domed cover
has an applied rim in silver-gilt with scrolling
foliate decoration and set with stones. The finial is
a silver-gilt cross set with stones.

33. CHALICE AND PATEN
1928
Gold, precious and semi-precious stones
Chalice h.23.3 w.15
Paten d.16.2
Inscribed: 'MADE FROM OLD GOLD
PRESENTED BY THE PARISHIONERS OF
VALLEY AND NEW FARM 1928. FATHER
D.M. O'KEEFE ADM.'
St Patrick's Catholic Church, Brisbane

The bowl has a calyx decorated with panels of
fruiting vine motif and set with stones. The
hexagonal stem is decorated with a repeated Gothic
fenestration motif and a band set with stones at the
juncture with foot. The compressed spherical knop
has lozenge-shaped bosses set with stones in deep
circular bezels with beaded circular surrounds. The
sexfoil foot is applied with a cross set with stones
and six fleur-de-lis motifs, from each of which

depends an applied strip of twisted gold wire. A
stone is set at each end of the wire. The vertical
edge of the sexfoil base has a band of open
quatrefoil pattern.
The circular paten is slightly dished.

34. MONSTRANCE
1928
Gold, precious and semi-precious stones, paste,
enamel plaques
H.78.5 w.38.5
Inscribed: 'FACTUM EX ORNAMENTIS
AUREIS A FIDELIBUS OBLATIS
MCMXXVIII'
St Stephen's Catholic Cathedral, Brisbane
Note: Made from gold and jewellery donated by
Queenslanders for presentation to the planned, but
never completed, Holy Name Cathedral, Brisbane.

The glazed roundel for the Host is surrounded by a
band embellished with a sexfoil pattern and set
with stones. Behind this extend the four arms of a
cross, each terminal set with an enamel medallion
depicting a devotional image. Behind encircling
bands of decoration, wavy rays extend. The
hexagonal stem has twelve panels of chased Gothic
fenestration and a band set with stones at the
juncture with foot. The compressed spherical knop
has lozenge-shaped bosses, set with stones, in deep
circular bezels. The trumpet foot is applied with six
fleur-de-lis motifs from each of which depends an
applied strip of twisted gold wire. A stone is set at
each end of the wire. The stepped sexfoil base is set
with stones and has two pierced bands of quatrefoil
pattern. The whole is surmounted by a cross finial
set with stones.

35. CROZIER
1929
Silver, metal, wood
H.177
Inscribed: 'To Henry Le Fanu Archbishop of Perth
from The Sisters of the Sacred Advent 1929'
Society of the Sacred Advent, Brisbane

The plain head terminates in an outward curve
with applied beads encircling a cross patée convex.
The capital of the shaft has a chased band of
basket-weave pattern below which is a tapered knop
decorated with coats-of-arms. The wooden shaft is
in three parts, with shaped silver bands at the junctures, and has a pointed metal tip.

36. PECTORAL CROSS
1929
Gold, amethysts
L.12.8 w.8.8
Inscribed: 'PRESENTED TO RT. REV. J. BYRNE
D.D. ON HIS APPOINTMENT AS FIRST
BISHOP OF TOOWOOMBA BY THE PRIESTS
OF THE ARCHDIOCESE OF BRISBANE
13.8.29'
Catholic Diocesan Archives, Toowoomba,
Queensland

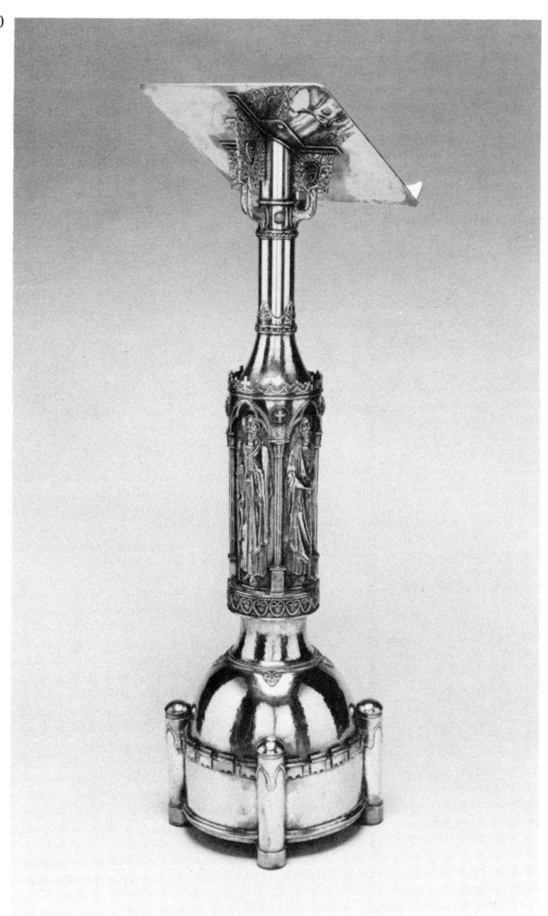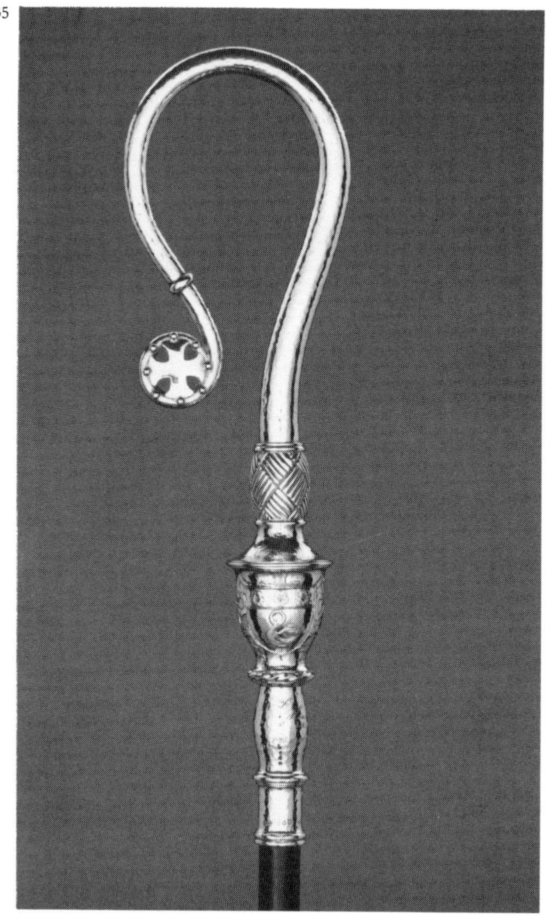

The obverse surface of the cross is applied with
scrolling twisted wire and granules and set with
five faceted amethysts. The reverse has a hinged reliquary at the intersection of the arms.

37. CROZIER
1929
Silver, semi-precious stones
H.188
Inscribed: 'PRESENTED TO RT. REV. DR. J.
BYRNE BY CHILDREN OF SCHOOLS OF
CHRISTIAN BROTHERS AND SISTERS OF
MERCY, IPSWICH'
Catholic Diocesan Archives, Toowoomba,
Queensland

The outer surface of the head is crocketed, its
inward curve terminating in an encircled cross set
with stones and attached to the stem by a long
scroll. The capital of the shaft has a knop with
convex fluting, below which is a compressed
spherical knop, applied with four decorated
roundels. The silver shaft is in three parts,
terminating in a tip with convex fluting.

Gordon Holdsworth—Hester,
Western Australia
B.England 1886 arr.1900 d.1965

38. ALTAR CROSS
c.1920
Copper, brass, enamel, moonstones
H.60.5 w.35.1
Inscribed: 'Presented to St. Paul's Cathedral in
loving memory of Caroline Mitchell—wife of W.B.
Mitchell. Born Bunbury Jan. 19th 1847 Died Aug.
9th 1918. By her Daughters Ente & Amy'
St Boniface's Anglican Cathedral, Bunbury,
Western Australia

The upper arms of the copper cross have brass
terminals. At the juncture of the arms is a square
brass panel set with a small enamelled boss and
applied at the rim with scrolling wire supporting
four cabochon moonstones. The cross rests on a
compressed spherical brass knop over a trumpet
foot, in copper, which is attached to four brass
cushion feet resting on a square flat copper base.

39. METROPOLITICAL CROSS
c.1920
Copper, silver, lapis lazuli, enamel
H.190.5
St George's Anglican Cathedral, Perth

The four arms of the copper cross have embossed
silver panels depicting a stylized fruiting vine. At
the intersection of the arms is a circular painted

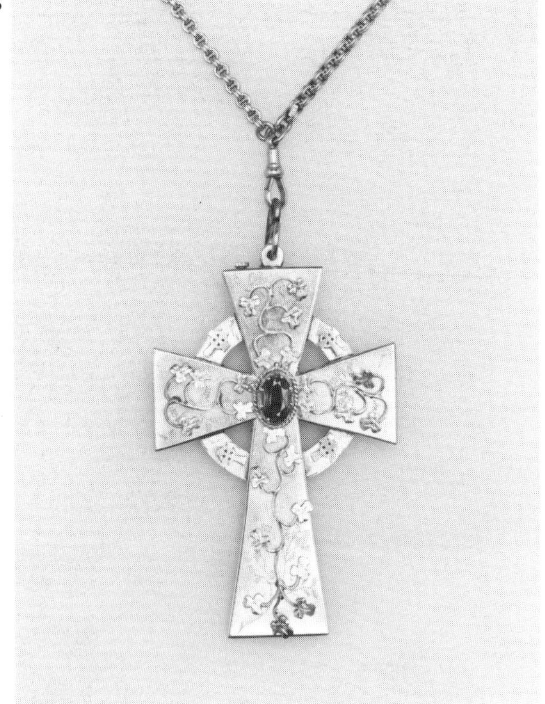

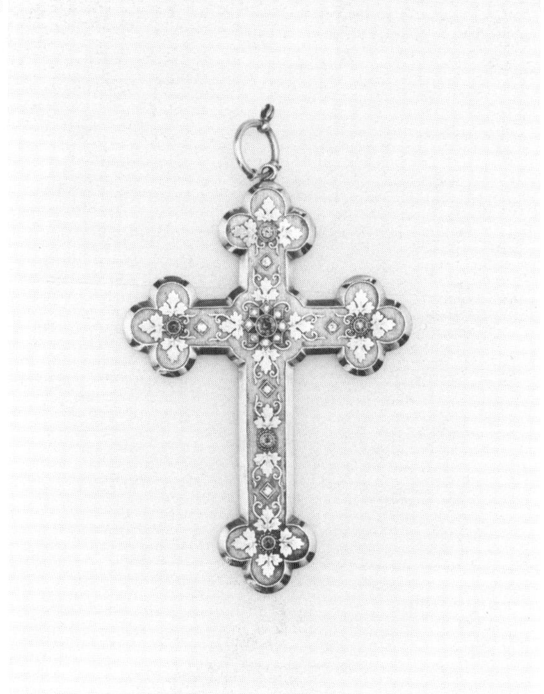

enamel depicting St George encircled by an embossed silver band with interlaced motif. At the juncture of the arms are four stylized fruiting vine
insets. The reverse is set with a small enamelled
boss, applied silver wire and leaf and fleur-de-lis
motifs in silver. The cross is set on copper stem
with applied silver wire and fleur-de-lis motifs. The
copper knop has a silver band of openwork depicting a fruiting vine and set with cabochon stones.
The wooden staff is decorated with bands of copper
with applied silver wire.

40. LECTERN
1922
Brass, enamel
H.140.7
St Paul's Anglican Church, Bridgetown,
Western Australia
Note: The lectern won a medal at the British Em-
pire Exhibition, Wembley, 1924

The book rest is supported by four arms, three in
the form of a fruiting vine (with fruit enamelled),
which rise from a cylindrical stem. This has four
embossed panels, each depicting a male saint,
recessed within Gothic niches. Betweeen each of
these is set a circular enamel depicting the saint's
emblem. The whole is set on a domed castellated
base, on four cylindrical feet.

41. CIBORIUM
c.1943
Silver
H.20.5 d.9.2
Inscribed: 'In memory of Mary Ann Spencer NAN
1846–1943'
St Boniface's Anglican Cathedral, Bunbury,
Western Australia

The bowl rises to a broad band of applied repeated
leaf motifs at its rim. The tapering cylindrical stem
is applied with twisted wire at its juncture with
the bowl and the foot. The base of the stem is
decorated with applied scrolling wire and beads.
The domed foot has a circular base. The conical
cover is surmounted by a cross finial.

William Mark-Melbourne
B.1868 d.1966

42. PROCESSIONAL CROSS
1921
Brass, silver, copper, enamel, wood
H.216 w.42.5
Inscribed: 'A.M.D.G. A THANK OFFERING
FROM L.H.S. FEST. ST. MICH: & ALL
ANGELS 1921'
All Saints' Anglican Church, Geelong, Victoria

The brass surface of the cross is applied with silver

42

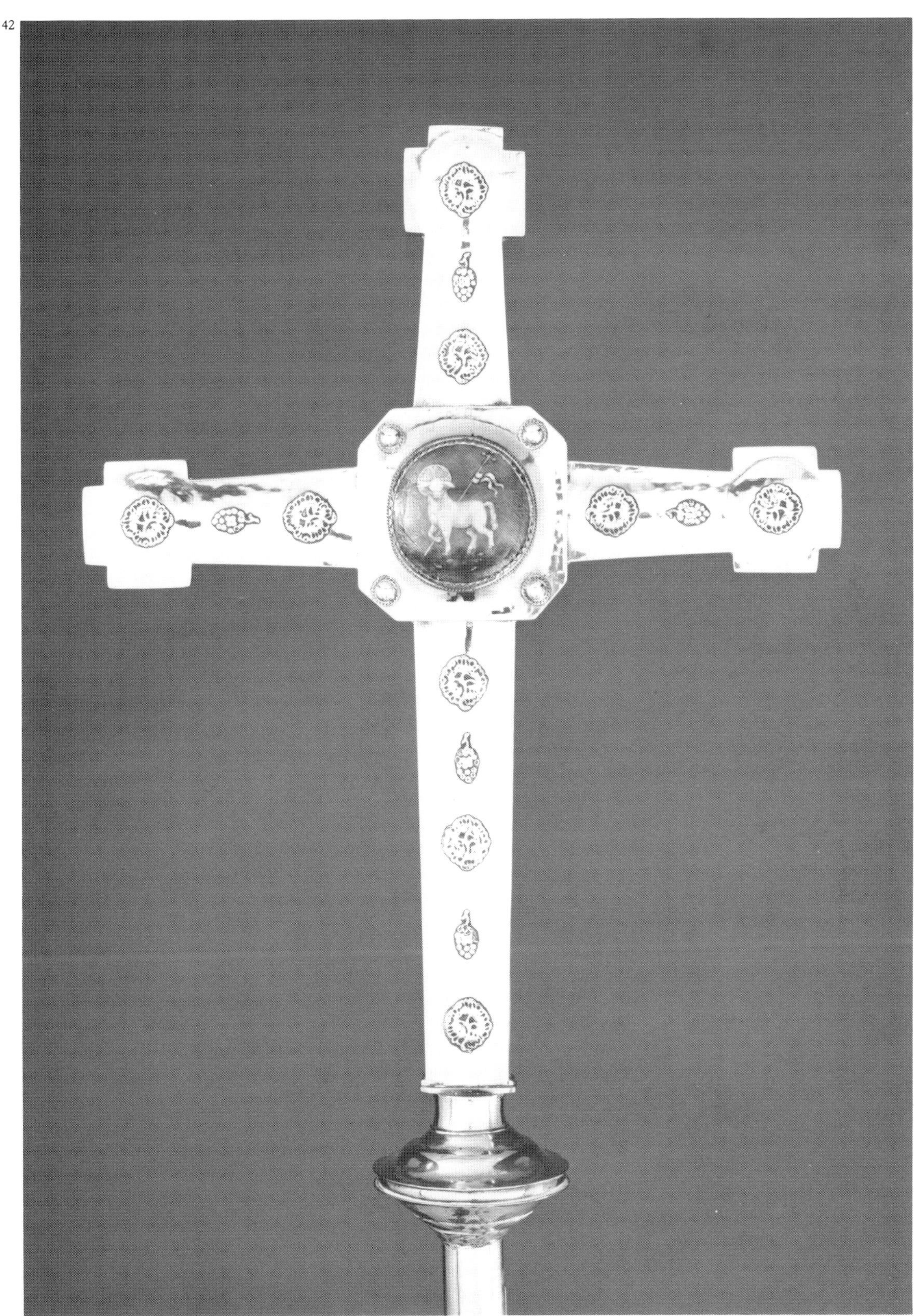

leaf and grape motifs. There is a circular painted enamel depicting an *Agnus Dei* at the intersection of the stepped arms. The reverse is similarly decorated except that the central enamel depicts a pelican in its piety. The lower arm rests above a compressed spherical knop below which a brass ferrule encircles the top of the wooden shaft.

43. CHALICE AND PATEN
Designed by Edward Spencer
1923
Gold, precious and semi-precious stones
Chalice h.21.6 w.10.9
Paten d.11.6
Inscribed: Chalice 'To ERNEST SELWYN HUGHES, Parish Priest from the parishioners of St. Peter's Church, Melbourne, in memory of thirty years work. 1894–1923' Paten 'TO CANON E.S. HUGHES FROM THE MEMBERS AND COMMITTEE OF THE E.M.C.C. 1920'
St Peter's Anglican Church, East Melbourne
Literature: The Sun News-Pictorial, 24 February 1923, p.27, illus.
Ewing 1947, p.5, cat.3

The bowl is set on a richly chased, tapering cylindrical stem set with stones. The spherical knop has four circular bosses set with medallions separately depicting a kangaroo, fire, dolphins and birds. The hexagonal foot is chased with a repeated sailing ship motif and a repeated gateway motif over a stylized representation of the sea. The vertical edge of the circular base has a band of pierced decoration depicting a flowering vine. The whole is supported on four pierced panels, set with stones and depicting the Tree of Life, which are inset into the rim of the base and connected to the foot by four buttresses.

The circular paten has a central depression embossed with a cross patée convex. The flat rim is engraved with vine leaf and grape motifs.

44. WAFER BOX
c.1924
Silver, gold, ivory, enamel, moonstones
L.18.9 w.12.6 h.6
Inscribed: 'TO THE GLORY OF GOD In Loving Memory of ALAN WILSON MOREY Born Mar. 1st 1893. S.P.S.C. 1906-1911 Adelaide University 1912-1914, Rhodes Scholar 1914. Lieut. 11th Ryl Scots, Sept 1914. Wounded at Loos Sept 1915. Twice mentioned in dispatches Military Cross. Joined R.F.C. Nov. 1915 Killed in Action Jan 24th 1918 "and underneath 'Were the Everlasting Arms'' '
Anglican Diocese of Adelaide
Literature: The Argus, 28 March 1924, p.13

The four sides of the box have embossed borders and applied twisted wire. The front is decorated with a cabochon moonstone and two circular painted enamels, one depicting a kangaroo, the other, two dolphins. The back has two circular painted enamels, one depicting a bird, the other fire, and two hinge mounts. Each of the other two sides has a handle attached. A turned ivory pillar is set at each of the four corners of the box, connecting foot to rim. The lid has an applied border, two pierced hinges and an applied gold dove within a decorative circular band incorporating four cabochon moonstones.

45. ALTAR CROSS AND CANDLESTICKS
1924
Silver, brass, copper, enamel, moonstones
Cross h.69 w.32.8
Candlesticks h.37.5 w.16
Inscribed: Illegible
Christ Church Anglican Cathedral, Newcastle, New South Wales

The reverse of the cross is fabricated from brass sheet. The obverse is applied with silver panels engraved with a fruiting vine which terminate in roundels with circular enamels, each depicting the symbol of an Evangelist, framed by an applied interlacing pattern. A circular painted enamel, at the intersection of the arms, depicts an *Agnus Dei*; this is framed by a band set with twelve cabochon moonstones and decorated with cloisonné enamel. The cross rests on a pierced copper knop of stylized foliage beneath which is a brass trumpet foot, with two applied silver bands decorated with linear pattern, set on six cushion feet.

The silver socket of the candlestick has a decorative band of wavy linear pattern below its rim. The silver drip tray is supported on a hexagonal brass stem resting on a pierced copper knop of stylized foliage. The brass trumpet foot has an applied silver band decorated with wavy linear pattern and is set on three cushion feet.

46. 'BOOK OF GOLD'
c.1924
Gold, enamel, amethysts, moonstones
L.24.9 w.21.3
Christ Church Anglican Cathedral, Newcastle, New South Wales

The covers of the memorial book are encased in gold and are applied with pierced hinges attached to the spine. The front cover is centrally applied with a circular enamel depicting a dove. This is encircled twice by beaded wire and there are four cabochon amethysts set at the edge of the outer circle, from which radiate four tapering enamelled arms, each terminating in a gold crown and a cabochon moonstone.

47. CHALICE AND PATEN
c.1924
Gold, precious and semi-precious stones, pearls, enamel
Chalice h.22.1 w.13.1
Paten d.14.8
Christ Church Anglican Cathedral, Newcastle, New South Wales
Note: Made from gold and jewellery presented by

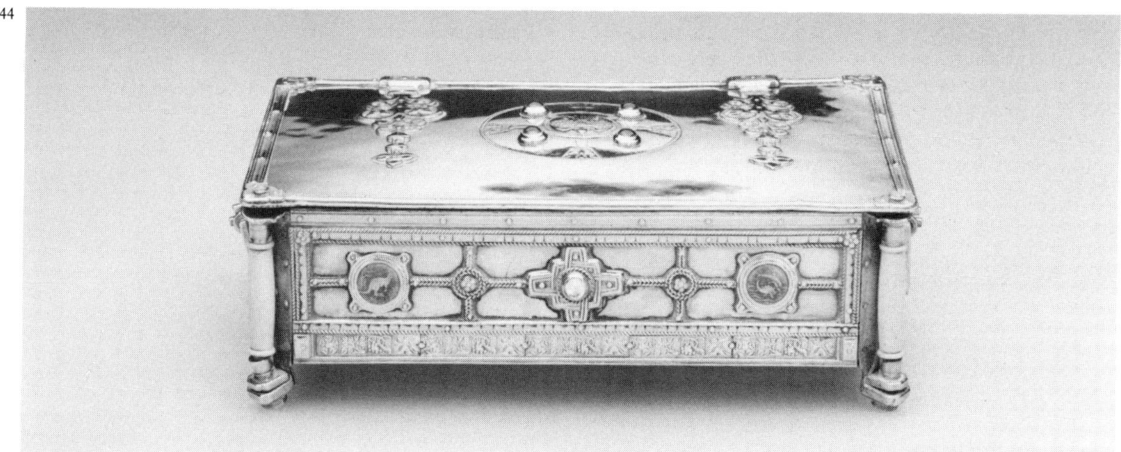

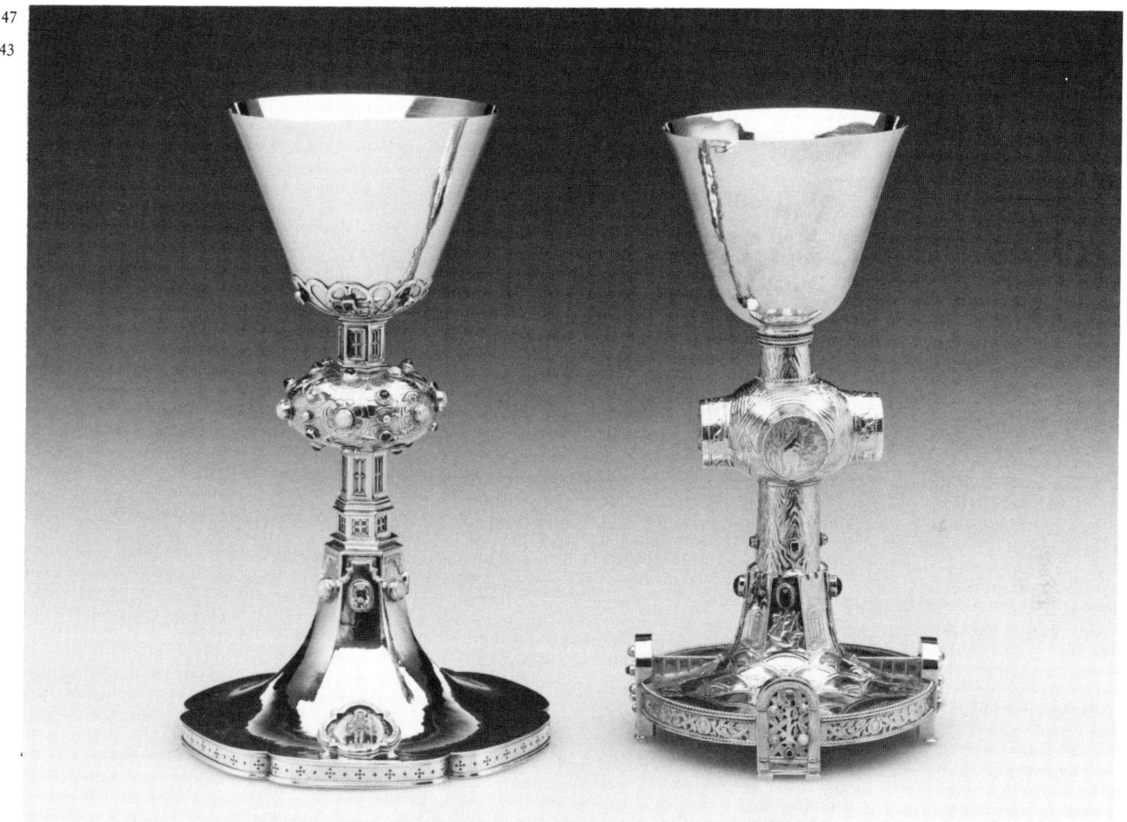

the relatives and friends of those who had died in
the first world war
Literature: Ewing 1947, p.6, cat.12a

The bowl of the chalice has a scalloped and
patterned calyx set with stones. The hexagonal
stem is decorated with a repeated fenestration
motif. The compressed spherical knop is chased
with stylized floral motifs and set with stones. The
hexagonal foot is set with stones below the
juncture with stem and has a quatrefoil enamel
depicting St Michael near its rim. The sexfoil base
has a pierced vertical edge.

The circular paten is centrally applied with a
medallion depicting a sailing ship. The rim is
engraved with a grape and vine leaf motif and set
with stones.

48. DEAN'S STAFF
c.1927
Silver, enamel
H.119.5 w.13.5
St Paul's Anglican Cathedral, Melbourne

The head of the staff is a quatrefoil composed of
four engraved silver arches joined by four engraved
rectangular segments applied with cloisonné enamel
panels. Each segment is surmounted by a silver
lunette and a cabochon moonstone within an
octagonal silver surround. This outer frame is connected to a central enamelled quatrefoil, which is
applied with the Anglican diocesan arms of
Melbourne in enamel on the obverse and depicts
the cross of St George on the reverse.

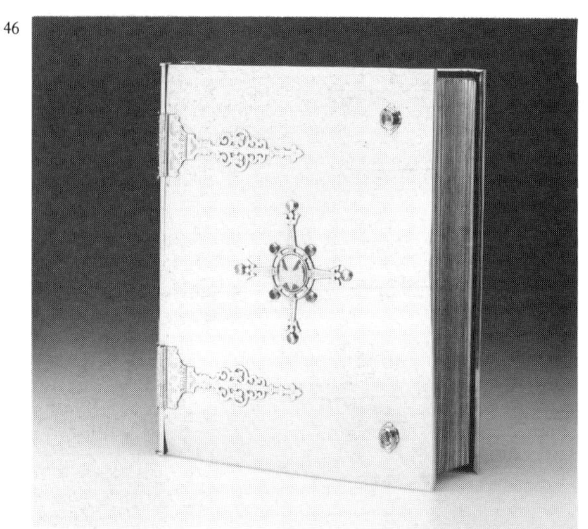

46

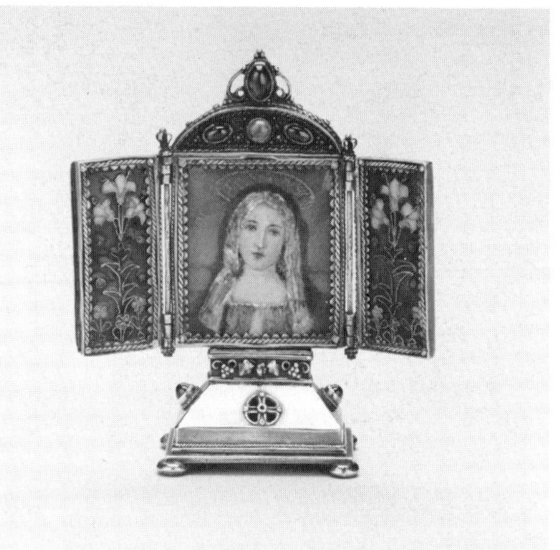

51

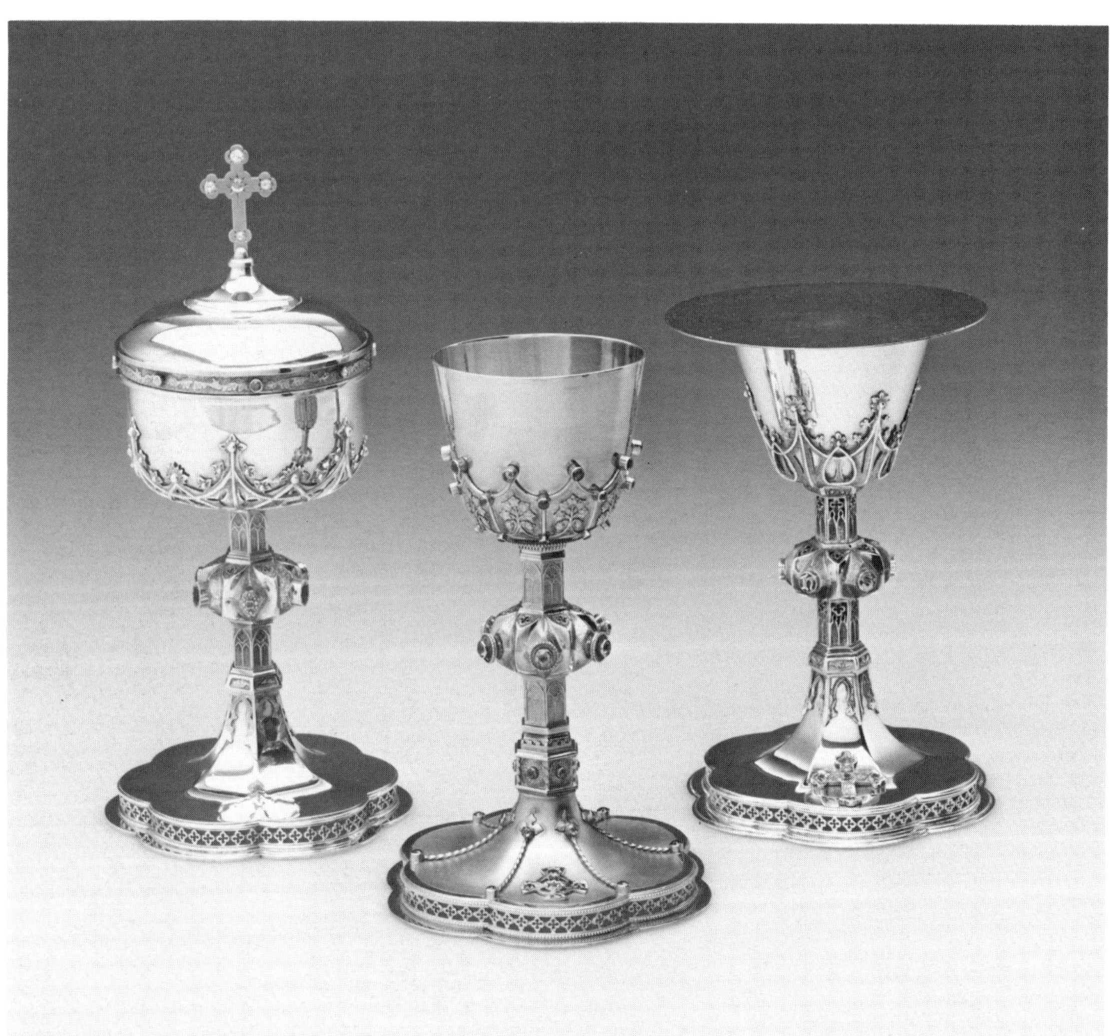

32 33 31

39

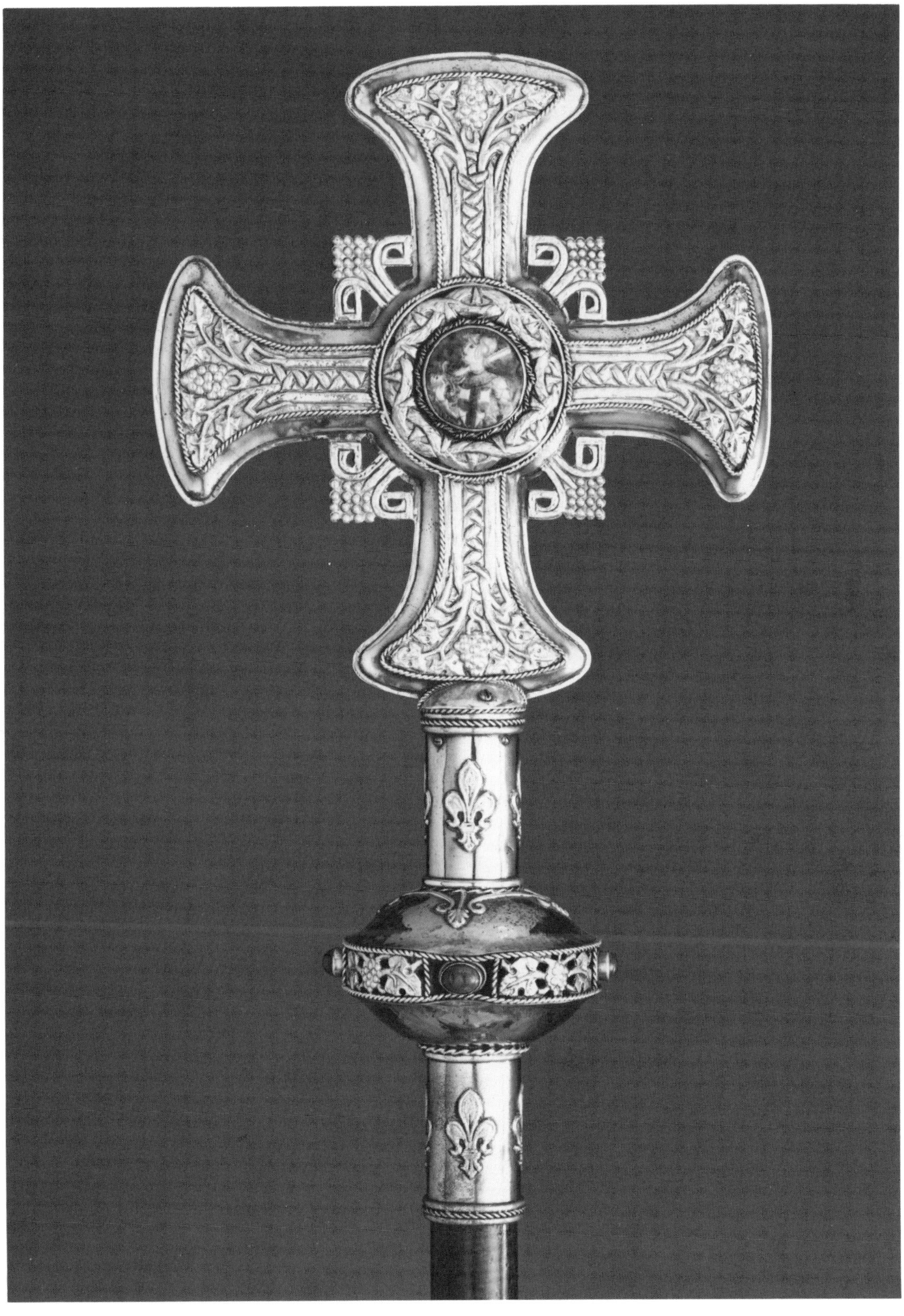

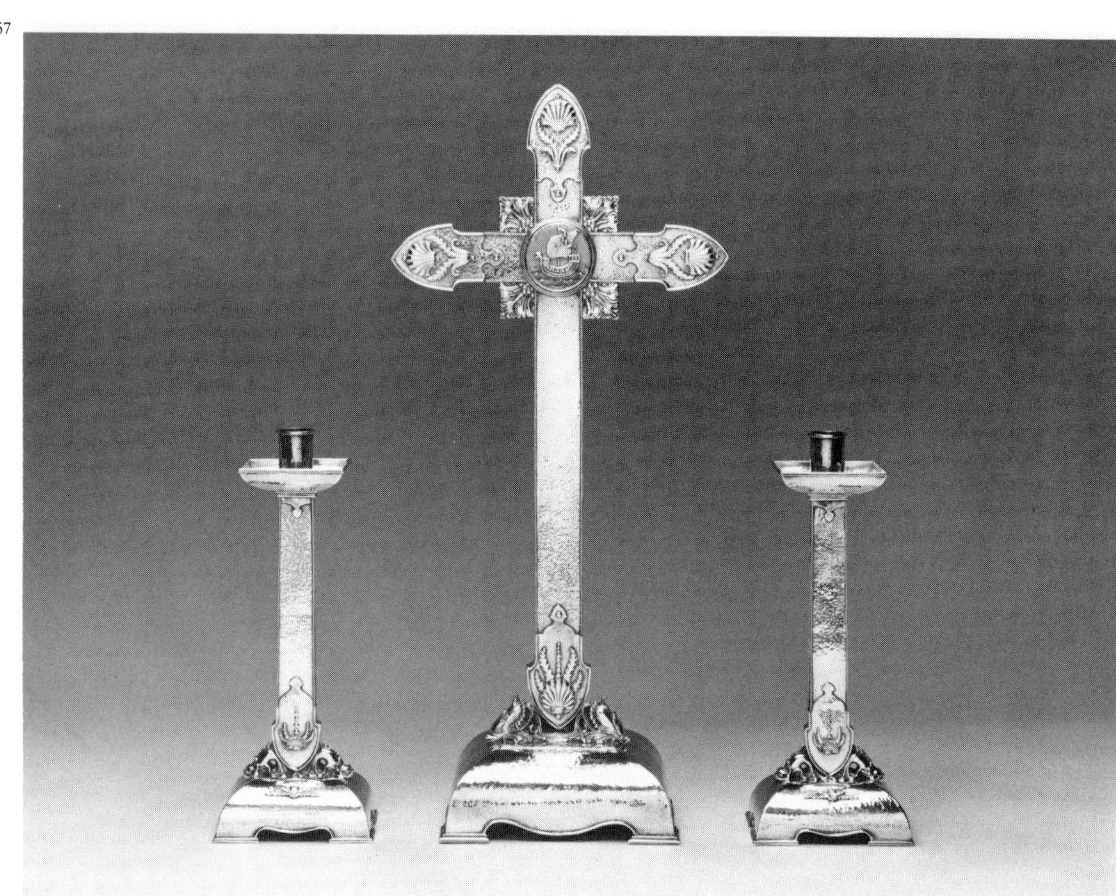

57

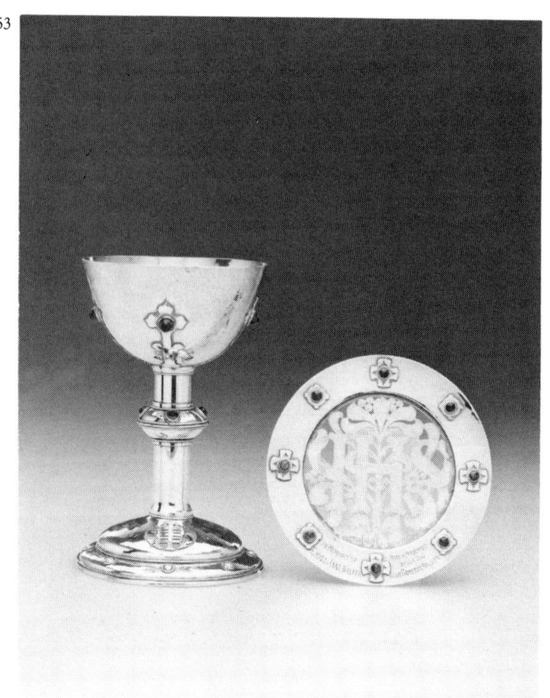

53

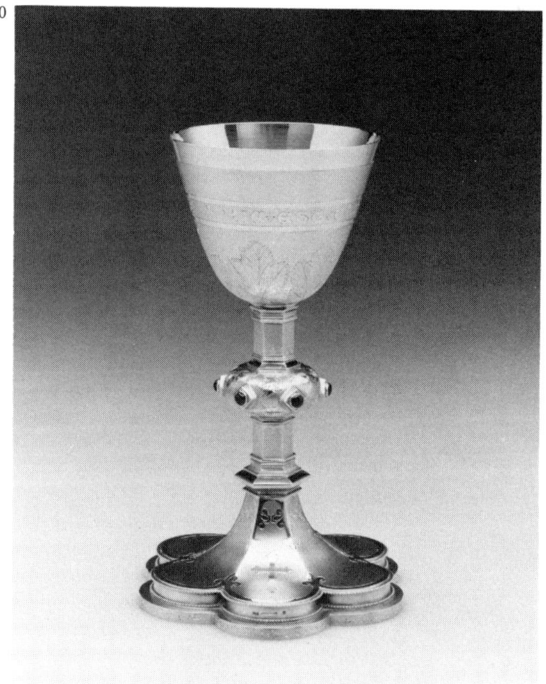

50

49. PROCESSIONAL CROSS
Designed by Louis Williams
c.1931
Silver, gold, enamel, wood, moonstone
H.225.5 w.39.8
Inscribed: 'TO THE GLORY OF GOD IN
LOVING MEMORY OF CANON FREDERIC
EVELYN STURT SNODGRASS, M.A. BORN
4 FEBRUARY 1866—PASSED TO A HIGHER
SERVICE 20 DECEMBER 1929 THIS CROSS
WAS PRESENTED TO ST. PAUL'S
CATHEDRAL MELBOURNE'
St Paul's Anglican Cathedral, Melbourne
Literature: Rogan 1976, p.16, cat.135

Each of the upper arms of the cross terminates in a
fleur-de-lis. The surface is applied with geometric
motifs connecting five circular enamels. The central
enamel depicts an *Agnus Dei* set within a circular
silver frame embossed with radiating lines. Each of
the other four enamels depicts a symbol of an
Evangelist. There are four cast stylized fruiting vine
insets at the juncture of the arms. The crossed
swords of St Paul, in gold, are applied to the base
of the cross. On the reverse, at the juncture of the
arms, is a circular enamel depicting a pelican in its
piety. The cross rests on a tapering cylindrical knop,
below which is an octagonal knop, with two
horizontal arms, set with a cabochon moonstone.
The staff is in wood with a silver tip.

FIDLER & KENWRICK—Adelaide
c.1921-35

50. CHALICE AND PATEN
1921
Gold, garnets
Chalice h.24.3 w.15.3
Paten d.15
Inscribed: 'Ex donis fidelium Archidiocesis
Adelaidensis Illmo. et Revmo Roberto Gulielmo
Spence Archiepiscopo ejusdem Archidiocesis. 22
Februarii 1921.'
St Francis Xavier Catholic Cathedral, Adelaide
Note: Both chalice and paten bear the retail mark of
J. Maly & Co.
Literature: The Australian Manufacturing Jewellers',
Watchmakers' and Opticians' Gazette 18, 12,
August 1921, p.13, illus.

The bowl of the chalice has a calyx of engraved
vine leaves and is engraved with the legend 'HIC
EST ENIM CALIX SANGUINIS MEI.' The
hexagonal stem has a compressed spherical knop
which is engraved with vine leaves and grapes and
has six lozenge-shaped bosses set with cabochon
garnets. The hexagonal stem on moulded sexfoil
base, is engraved with fleur-de-lis motifs and a
cross.
    The circular paten has a centrally applied IHS
monogram within an engraved decorative band
bordered by two circles of applied wire.

Caroline (Carrie) Francis—Melbourne

51. TRIPTYCH
c.1925
Silver, enamel, garnets, moonstone
H.11.2 w.9.6
National Gallery of Victoria
Purchased 1966
1375.5
Literature: H.V.M. Roberts, 'MISS CARRIE
FRANCIS'S JEWELLERY', The Studio 89, 387,
pp.328–9, illus.

Two silver doors, each decorated with a central
cross motif and trefoils at each corner, open to
show three enamel panels—the central panel in
painted enamel depicts the Virgin Mary, the left
and right panels, in cloisonné enamel, depict lilies
and other flowers. The central panel is surmounted
by a lunette set with two cabochon garnets and a
cabochon moonstone. Above this is a cabochon
garnet set within an oval bezel supported by scrolling wire. A band of fruiting vine motif is applied
below the triptych at the junction with the base,
which is composed of four sloping sides, two set
with cabochon garnets and one decorated with a
cross motif. The whole rests on four cushion feet.

E. Priora—Sydney
Active c.1911-32

52. PECTORAL CROSS
1930
Gold, diamonds, rubies
L.11.5 w.7.9
Inscribed: 'Gulielmo Hayden Archiepiscopo
Hobarten Sacerdotes. Diocesis Wilc.—Forben Me
Donum Dederunt, Anno 1930'
St Mary's Catholic Cathedral, Hobart

The arms of the cross have trefoil terminals and are
applied with vine leaf and scrolling motifs and set
with six rubies and thirteen diamonds. The reverse
a reliquary at the intersection of the arms.

Alan Cameron Walker—Hobart
B.1864 d.1931

53. CHALICE AND PATEN
1931
Silver, amethysts, glass
Chalice h.22.2 w.14.1
Paten d.16.7
Inscribed: Chalice 'IN MEMORY OF EMMA
JANE WALKER MADE & PRESENTED BY
HER SON ALAN CAMERON WALKER
MARCH 1931' Paten 'IN MEMORY OF EMMA
JANE WALKER MADE & PRESENTED BY
HER SON ALAN CAMERON WALKER'
St David's Anglican Cathedral, Hobart

The bowl of the chalice has a calyx composed of
four applied fleur-de-lis motifs, each set with a

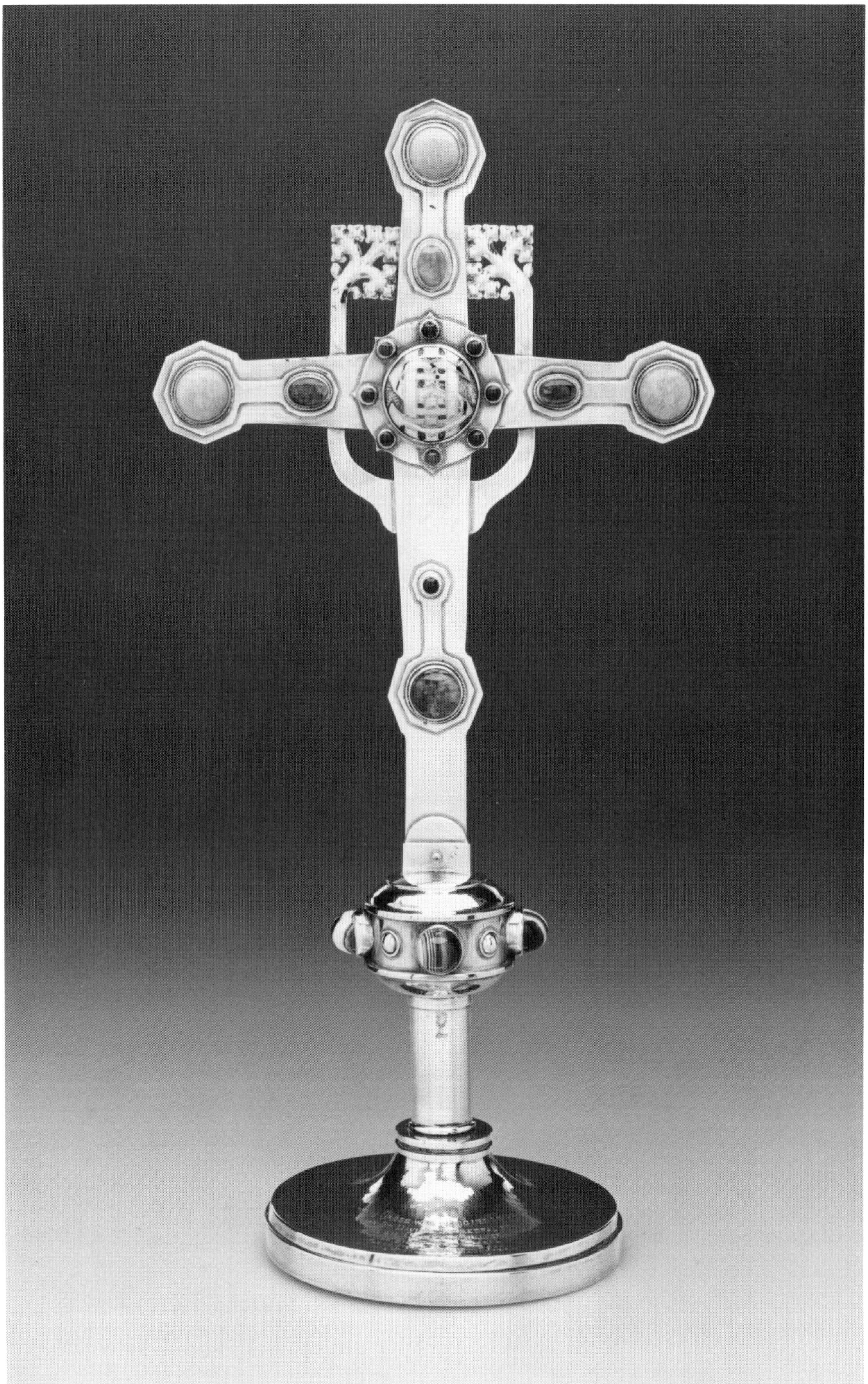

cabochon amethyst. The cylindrical stem has a
compressed spherical knop applied with twisted
wire and set with four cabochon amethysts. The
domed foot is applied with a silver cross and a
silver IHS monogram and its rim is set with eight
silver bosses.

The centre of the circular paten has a pierced
IHS motif interlaced with stylized foliage and
covered with glass. The rim is applied with four
crosses alternating with four quatrefoils, each set
with cabochon amethysts.

54. ALTAR CROSS
c.1931
Silver, gold, semi-precious stones
H.63 w.31
Inscribed: 'THIS CROSS WAS DESIGNED AND
MADE FOR ST. DAVID'S CATHEDRAL BY
ALAN CAMERON WALKER WHO DIED
DEC 12TH 1931 PRESENTED ON DEC 12TH
1932 BY HIS WIDOW AND DAUGHTER'
St David's Anglican Cathedral, Hobart

The tapered upper arms of the cross have hexagonal
terminals, each set with two large cabochon stones
connected by applied silver panels. The lower arm is
similarly decorated with a large cabochon amethyst
and small cabochon garnet. There is a boss, with
an IHS monogram applied in gold, surrounded by
eight cabochon garnets, at the intersection of the
arms. Below this, a flat stylized vine branch rises
from each side of the stem and passes behind the
horizontal arms to rejoin the upper arm. The cross
is secured above a knop decorated with four
cabochon stones and four silver bosses. The cylindrical stem below rests on a low trumpet foot with
circular base.

Harold Sargison—Hobart
B.1885 d.1983

55. MONSTRANCE
Designed by Alan C. Walker
1932
Gold, precious and semi-precious stones
H.64.2 w.30.8
Inscribed: 'When the Illustrious and Most Rev.
William Hayden, D.D., Archbishop of Hobart,
received and blessed this Monstrance of 15-ct. gold
for his Cathedral on the Feast of Christ the King,
1932, the hearts of his devoted people rejoiced that
their little treasures, which were solely used in its
construction—associations of their joys, sorrows,
and their beloved dead—should find herein so
sacred a resting-place in the service of the Master'
St Mary's Catholic Cathedral, Hobart
Note: Drawing by Alan C. Walker lent by Miss J.
Sargison, Hobart

The monstrance is in the form of a cross with sun-
burst behind. The upper tapered arms have
hexagonal terminals, each of these has an applied
symbol set with stones—the upper bears a cross,
the left bears a symbol for Alpha, the right bears a
symbol for Omega. At the intersection of the arms,
the glazed roundel reserved for the Host is edged

with pearls which are framed by a decorative band
set with eight faceted stones. Emerging from
behind this are the four arms of a cross set with
stones, decorated with filigree and an applied Chi-
Rho set with stones. Four fruiting vine motifs are
inset at the juncture of the arms of the cross
proper. The lower arm is set with a cabochon stone
and pearls and rests on a spherical knop, with convex fluting, set with a band of eight cabochon
stones. Beneath this, an octagonal stem with
moulded foot rests on a plinth.

Andor Meszaros—Melbourne
B.Hungary 1900 arr.1939 d.1972

56. STATIONS OF THE CROSS
1942–70
Silvered bronze
D. 6.4
National Gallery of Victoria
Presented by the National Gallery Society of
Victoria 1961–73
366–372.5, D152/1969, D415/1972, D249/1973

Fourteen silvered bronze medallions, depicting the
stations of the cross, are mounted on rectangular
wooden plaques.

J.A. Linton—Perth
B.1904 d.1980

57. ALTAR CROSS AND CANDLESTICKS
c.1944–45
Silver, enamel
Cross h.71.3 w.33.4
Candlesticks h.38.2
Inscribed: Cross 'A.M.D.G. In Loving Memory of
Helen Gregory 1927–1942 Leonard C. Gregory
1891-1960'. Candlesticks 'In Loving Memory of
DUNCAN CHARLES FREDERICK GOOD
Squadron Leader R.A.F. Killed in Action 1941
Aged 25 Years'. 'In Loving Memory of
CHRISTOPHER MARSHALL GOOD Warrant
Officer R.A.A.F. Killed on Active Service 1945
Aged 21 Years'
St Jude's Anglican Church, Brighton,
South Australia
Literature: L. Andison, 'A History of Saint Jude's
Church, Brighton 1854–1979', vol I. (unpublished)
Note: Drawings lent by John Linton Esq.,
Maylands, Western Australia

The terminals of the four arms of the cross are
applied with scallop shell, air bubble and seaweed
motifs over applied shaped panels. At the intersection of the arms is a circular enamel depicting a
sailing ship. Four stylized fruiting vine motifs are
inset at the juncture of the arms. A cast stylized
dolphin is set on either side of the base of the
lower arm. This rests upon a high square base with
sloping sides, the rim shaped to delineate four feet.

Each of the candlesticks has a cylindrical socket,
with a drip tray, resting on a rectangular stem
which is applied at the base with scallop shell, air
bubble and seaweed motifs over an applied shaped
panel. A cast stylized dolphin is set on either side

of the base of the stem. This rests upon a high square base with sloping sides, the rim shaped to delineate four feet. Each base is applied with an Air Force insignia in silver.

58. WINE AND WATER CRUETS

c.1945
Silver, garnet
H.22
Inscribed: 'To the Glory of God & in Loving Memory of PETER TODD READ, Flying Officer R.A.A.F. 1920–1943''DORIS MURIEL READ 1893–1964'
St Jude's Anglican Church, Brighton,
South Australia
Literature: Andison, op.cit.

Each cruet has a tall, cylindrical spouted neck joined to a spherical body resting on a low concave foot. Bands of twisted wire are applied at the rim, the juncture of the neck and body, the rim of the foot and around the base of the domical cover. This has a flat projection to cover the spout and is surmounted by a ball finial. The body has an applied Air Force insignia. The handle has a wound wire handgrip, and in the case of the wine cruet, is set with a garnet.

59. FONT EWER

c.1945
Silver, enamel
H.26.2
Inscribed: 'A.D.M.G. *sic* IN MEMORIAM MABEL HARRIETTE JOHNSON 1867–1944'
St Jude's Anglican Church, Brighton,
South Australia
Literature: Andison, op.cit.

The tall jug, of gently sloping form, has its maximum diameter above the low circular foot. A band of flat and twisted wire is applied to the rim and around the body below the spout. A circular enamel depicting a sailing ship is set on either side of the body, between the two bands. An applied twisted wire encircles the foot near its rim. The handle has a wound wire handgrip.

Levinson—Perth

60. CHALICE

1947
Silver, amethysts
H.22.1 w.15.3
Inscribed: 'To the Glory of God and in Memory of Octavius Burt I.S.O. 1849–1940 A faithful Son of the Church who worshipped in the Cathedral-Church of St. George for nearly 80 years Nov 2nd, 1947.'
St George's Anglican Cathedral, Perth

The bowl is set on a hexagonal stem with a compressed spherical knop set with eight cabochon amethysts. The hexagonal foot has a sexfoil base.

Pellegrini & Co.—Australia
Established 1890

61. CHALICE AND PATEN

1948
Silver-gilt, diamond
Chalice h.20.1 w. 14.3
Paten c.15.1
Inscribed: 'TO THE REV. P.H. JONES FROM McCONNIE'S & DILLION'S 25'7'48'
St Patrick's Catholic Cathedral, Melbourne

The bowl of the chalice rests on a stem with a lobed knop. The trumpet foot, on a circular base, has a chased design in imitation of fluting and lobing and an applied cross set with a stone.

The circular paten has a chased scalloped pattern radiating from a central cross motif.

Dan Flynn—Kyneton, Victoria
B.1909 d.1978

62. CHALICE

1949
Silver-gilt
H.17.2 w.12.1
Inscribed: 'IN MEMORY OF IGNATIUS & MARY FLYNN & FAMILY 1949'
Lent by Mrs B. Flynn, Kyneton, Victoria
Literature: The Tribune, 11 February 1954, illus. Rogan 1976, p.22, cat.208

The cast stem and sexfoil foot is in the form of the figure of Christ crucified to a tree on rocky ground. The bowl is held in His outstretched arms. The vertical edge of the sexfoil base has a pierced band of fruiting vine motif.

63. CROWN

c.1952
Gold, silver, diamonds, rubies, opals, pearls
H.9 w.11.5
St Joseph's Catholic Church, Leeton, New South Wales
Note: The crown was made for a statue of the Virgin Mary

The crown is composed of two circlets separated by six small crosses, five set with an opal, the sixth set with a diamond. Above each cross is a motif in silver and gold consisting of a group of four lilies surmounted by a celtic cross. Each motif is set with a garnet and pearls and one is also set with diamonds. Between each of these motifs is the small figure of an angel in gold.

64. CHALICE AND PATEN

c.1955
Gold, silver, silver-gilt
Chalice h.22.6 d.15.4
Paten d.15
Inscribed: 'DONATED BY THE FAMILY IN MEMORY OF THEIR PARENTS WILLIAM ANDREW KELLY, DEC. 25th 1945, MARY TERESA KELLY, DEC. 10th 1953. R.I.P.'
Sacred Heart Catholic Cathedral, Bendigo, Victoria

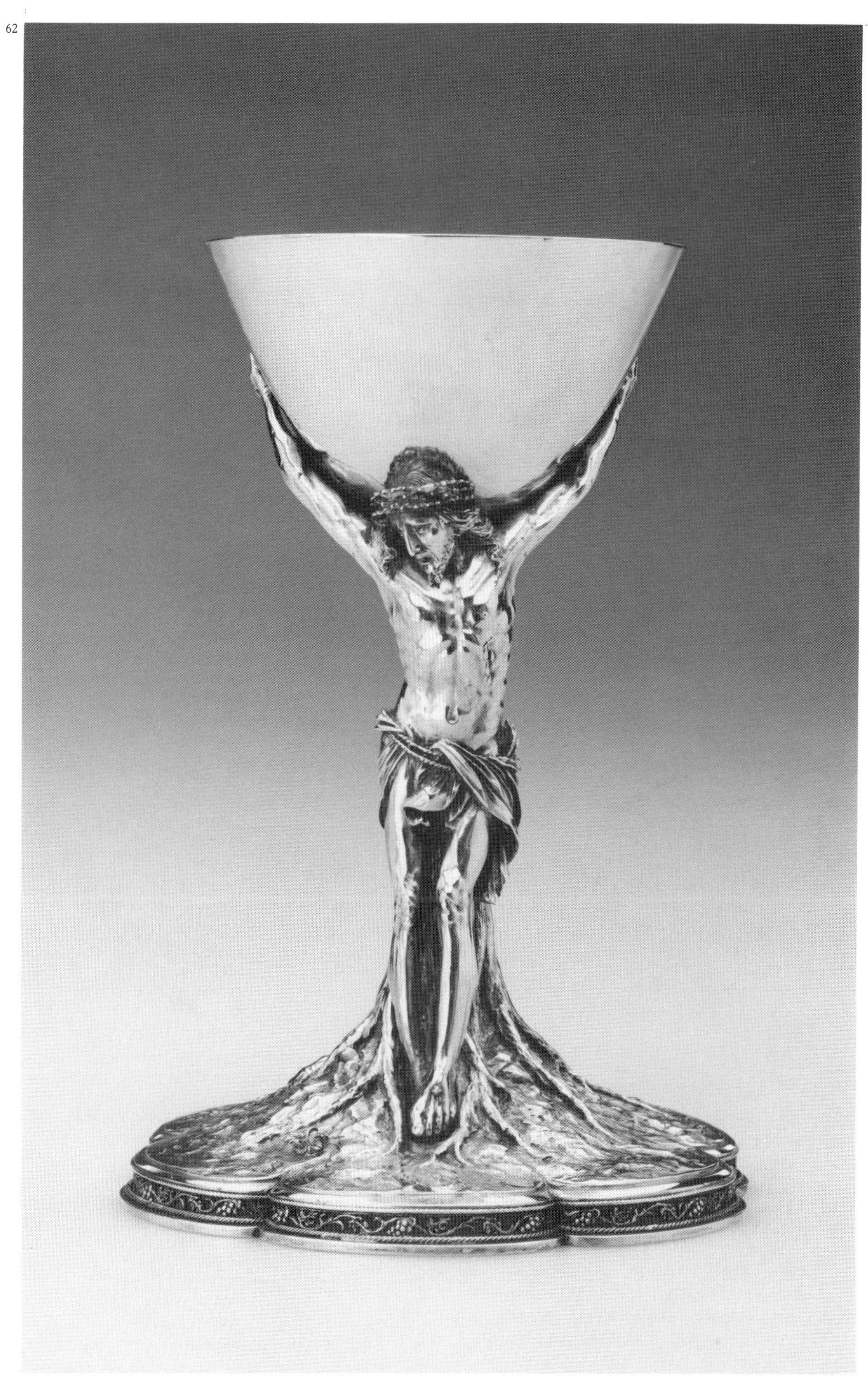

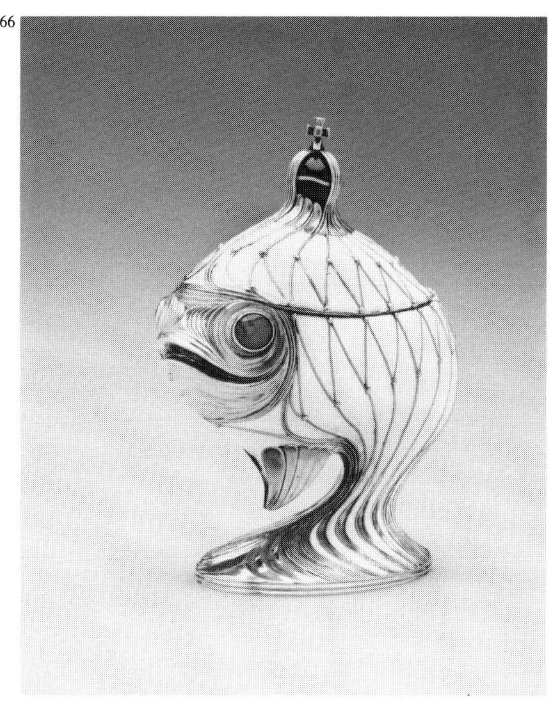

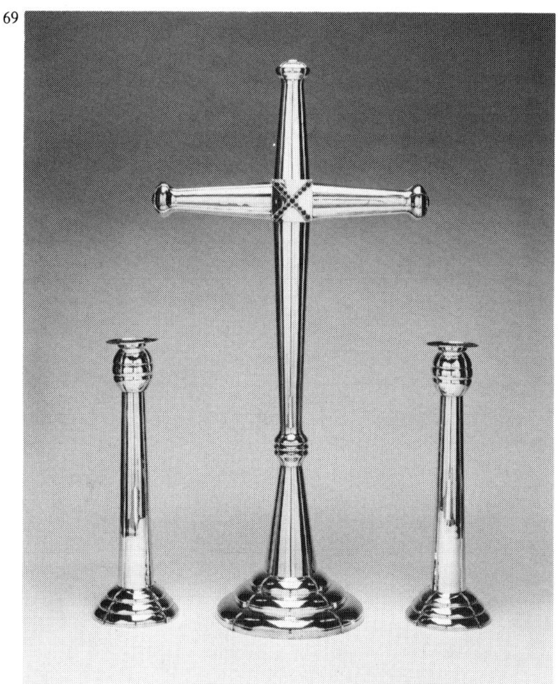

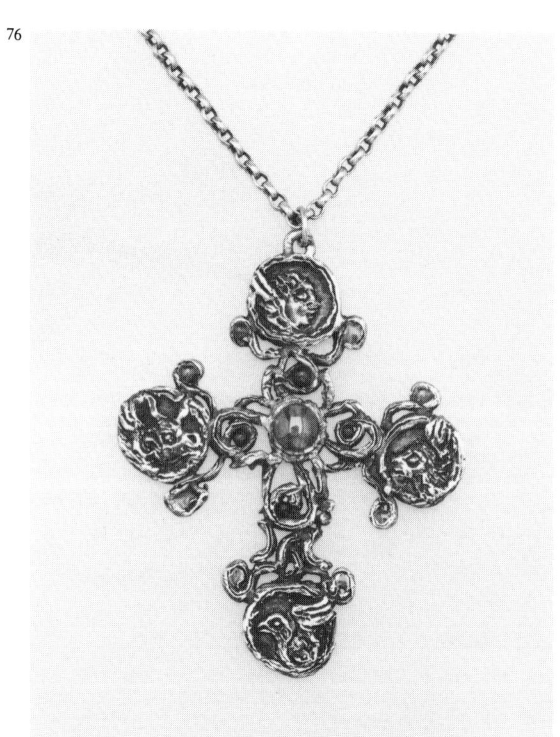

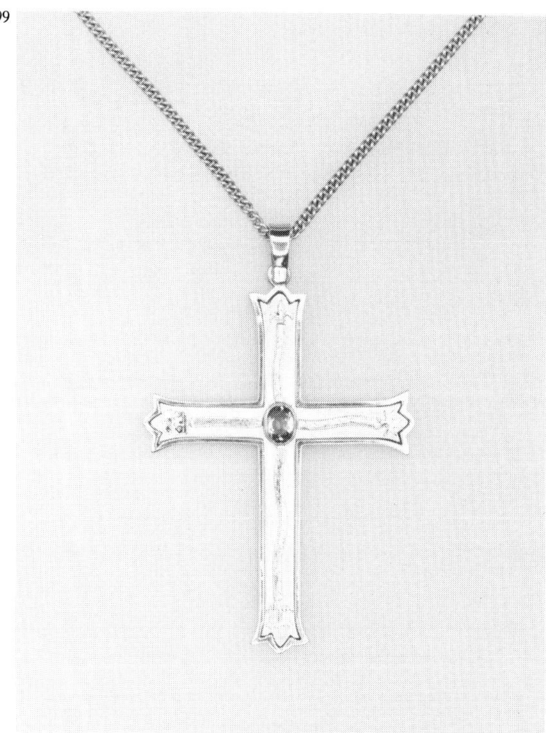

The stem of the chalice is composed of a stylized representation of the twelve apostles in silver, their hands forming the knop and their heads forming the calyx to the bowl. The gold conical foot is applied with a silver and gold medallion depicting the crucified Christ. The sloping rim has the engraved legend 'CHRISTI + MERUM + FITQUE + SANGUIS'. Twelve pairs of feet, in silver, protrude beneath the foot around its circumference.
The circular paten in silver-gilt is slightly dished.

65. CHALICE
1957
Gold, silver-gilt, diamonds, rubies
Chalice h.18.9 d.14.1
Paten d.14
Inscribed: 'ST. FRANCIS CHURCH, MELBOURNE BLESSED SACRAMENT FATHERS CENTENARY 1857–1957'
Catholic Diocese of Melbourne
Literature: Woman's Day, 10 August 1959, pp.38–9, illus.

The stem of the chalice is composed of six angels
blowing trumpets. The trumpets form a calyx to
the bowl, the heads form the knop, and their
robes, a hexagonal stem, the panels of which are set
with stones. Six pairs of feet protrude beneath the
robes and rest on the circular foot, the vertical rim
of which is applied with the legend 'SANCTUS
+ SANCTUS + SANCTUS', each letter set with
stones.

66. CIBORIUM
1960
Silver-gilt, enamel, opals, agate
H.11.2 w.9.5
Lent by Mrs B. Flynn, Kyneton, Victoria
Literature: Rogan 1976, p.22, cat. 208a

The ciborium is in the shape of a fish, its curved
tail forming the stem and foot. The white enamelled body is patterned with silver-gilt wire in imitation of scales. The face in silver-gilt is set with opal
eyes. The cover is surmounted by an agate orb
banded with silver-gilt and surmounted by a cross.

67. CROSS
c.1973
Silver, gold, ironwood
L.12 w.9
Lent by Mrs B. Flynn, Kyneton, Victoria

The cross, formed in wood, has tapering arms. The
intersection is set with a semi-abstract motif incorporating a small chalice, the gold bowl of which is
supported by curved lengths of wire. The whole is
rimmed in silver.

J.W. Steeth & Son—Melbourne
1945–70
(J.W. Steeth established 1917)

68. CHALICE
1954
Gold, diamonds, rubies
H.21.5 d.15.4
Inscribed: 'IN LOVING MEMORY OF MY
DEAR WIFE IRENE ANN O'CONNOR
WHO DIED, 15th Dec. 1952. JOHN O'CON-
NOR' 'ST. FRANCIS CHURCH
MELBOURNE. 6.9.54'
Catholic Diocese of Melbourne

The bowl is inscribed with the legend 'CALICEM
SALUTARIS ACCIPIAM ET NOMEN DOMINI
INVOCABO + '. The cylindrical stem has a
compressed spherical knop with applied fruiting
vine motif and a Chi-Rho. The trumpet foot has
an applied cross set with stones.

69. ALTAR CROSS AND CANDLESTICKS
Designed by Louis Williams
c.1962
Silver, blue stones
Cross h.137 w.68
Candlesticks h.68

St Andrew's Anglican Church, Brighton, Victoria

The four arms of the cross are tapering cylinders
and the upper arms have shaped terminals. The
lower arm terminates in a ribbed knop above a
trumpet foot with stepped, domed base. A cross of
St Andrew in silver, set with blue stones, is applied
at the intersection of the arms. Four applied bands
of silver run the length of the arms, knop, foot
and base.

The drip pan of each candlestick has a ribbed
knop below. The stem is a tapering cylinder set on
a stepped, domed base. Four applied bands of silver
run the length of the whole.

70. CHALICE AND PATEN
Possibly designed by Louis Williams
c.1962
Silver, diamonds, paten with traces of gilding
Chalice h.23 d.14.4
Paten d.15.2
St Andrew's Anglican Church, Brighton, Victoria

The bowl of the chalice is engraved with leaves
which form crosses, stars and a Chi-Rho and rests
on a ribbed knop. A trumpet foot with stepped,
domed base bears a cross of St Andrew set with
stones. Engraved lines in imitation of the banding
on the cross and candlesticks (cat.69) run the
length of the foot and the base.

The circular paten is engraved with a Chi-Rho
and stars.

71. FLAGON
Possibly designed by Louis Williams
c.1962
Silver, silver-gilt
H.28 w.26
St Andrew's Anglican Church, Brighton, Victoria

The spouted bowl is engraved with leaves which
form crosses, stars and a Chi-Rho and rests on a
ribbed knop. The trumpet foot has a stepped,
domed base. There are engraved lines similar to
those on the chalice (cat.70). The conical lid, with
scalloped rim, is surmounted by a leaf-cross finial.

The ciborium has a shaped handle.

Matcham Skipper—Eltham, Victoria
B.1921

72. STATIONS OF THE CROSS:
CHRIST BEFORE PILATE
CHRIST MEETS HIS MOTHER
CHRIST IS STRIPPED
1961
Metal
L.77.5 w.54.5; l.79 w.57; l.79 w.55.5
Mary Immaculate Catholic Church, Ivanhoe,
Victoria

Each station of the cross is composed of a dished
rectangular panel with an irregularly shaped cast
panel centrally attached.

Emily Hope—Melbourne
B.1940 d. 1979

73. CHALICE AND PATEN
1962
Silver
Chalice h.21.6 d.12.8
Paten d.14.6
Lent by The Reverend Ian F. Brown, Melbourne

The bowl of the chalice rests above a cast silver
knop depicting two heads and a fruiting vine. Cast
symbols of the four Evangelists are individually
applied near the rim of the trumpet foot.
    The circular paten in silver-gilt is embossed with
the figure of a sheep and a repeated grape motif.

74. CHALICE AND PATEN
1963
Gold, silver-gilt, enamel, precious and semi-precious
stones, pearls
Chalice h.21.3 d.13.5
Paten d.13.9
Inscribed: 'This jewelled chalice and solid gold paten
were formed from The offering of Parishioners St.
Anselms Church, Middle Park 1963. For the
greater Glory of God in the Holy Mass'
St Anselm's Anglican Church, Middle Park,
Victoria
Note: Chalice bears the maker's mark of House of
Design

The bowl of the chalice rests on a tapered cylindrical stem, encircled with an applied band of floral
motifs. The cylindrical knop is set with stones and
pearls and an applied cross also set with stones and
pearls. The trumpet stem, on circular base, has an
applied motif depicting Christ in vestments, with
branches, set with stones, issuing from His body.
This applied motif has traces of enamelling.
    The circular paten is slightly dished.

75. CHALICE AND PATEN
1968
Silver, silver-gilt
Chalice h.12.3 d.14.7
Paten d.15.8
Inscribed: 'EMILY ME FECIT 1968 A.D. GLORIA
IN EXELCIS *sic* DEO'
The Society of St Francis, Brisbane

The bowl of the chalice rests on a stem, composed
of the cast figures of cockatoos, which rests on a
low circular foot.
    The circular paten, like the bowl of the chalice,
has a pronounced hammered surface.

76. CROSS
c.1970
Silver, enamel, opals, garnets
L.7.8 w.6.2
Lent by The Reverend Andrew St John, Melbourne
Literature: Rogan 1976, p.23, cat.213

Each arm of the cross terminates in a roundel,
depicting a symbol for one of the Four Evangelists,

with a blue enamel inlay on either side. An opal is
set at the intersection of the arms surrounded by
four cabochon garnets.

Allan Thomas—Melbourne
B.1931

77. ALTAR CROSS
1964
Silver-plate, opal, resin
H.93.3 w.67.5
St George's Anglican Church, East Ivanhoe,
Victoria

The tapering arms of the cross are each composed
of two sheets of silver plate enclosing molten metal
set with rough cut opals. The whole is set on a
rectangular acrylic base.

78. CHALICE
1964
Silver, opal, resin
Chalice h.26.5 d.11.7
St George's Anglican Church, East Ivanhoe,
Victoria

The cylindrical stem of the chalice is composed of
molten metal which forms a calyx to the bowl.
The conical foot has a circular acrylic base.

79. CIBORIUM
1964
Silver, opal, resin
H.31.5 d.11.7
St George's Anglican Church, East Ivanhoe,
Victoria

The cylindrical stem of the ciborium is composed
of molten metal which forms a calyx to the bowl.
The conical foot has a circular acrylic base. The
shallow conical cover is surmounted by a cross
finial.

John Hale—Adelaide
B.1927

80. WINE AND WATER CRUETS
1966
Silver, silver-gilt, garnet
H.22.2
Inscribed: Wine 'TO THE GLORY OF GOD
AND IN MEMORY OF LETTY MARJORIE
JOYCELYN CHARLES AND ALISON HORN
"HOFWYL" CRAFERS'. Water 'TO THE
GLORY OF GOD AND IN LOVING
MEMORY OF CHARLES AUSTIN HORN
AND HIS WIFE LETITIA REBECCA
"HOFWYL" CRAFERS'
Anglican Church of the Epiphany, Crafers,
South Australia

Each of the cruets has a hexagonal spouted body on
a protruding stepped hexagonal base. The domed
hexagonal cover is surmounted by a finial in the
form of a cross within a circle. The handle emerges

80

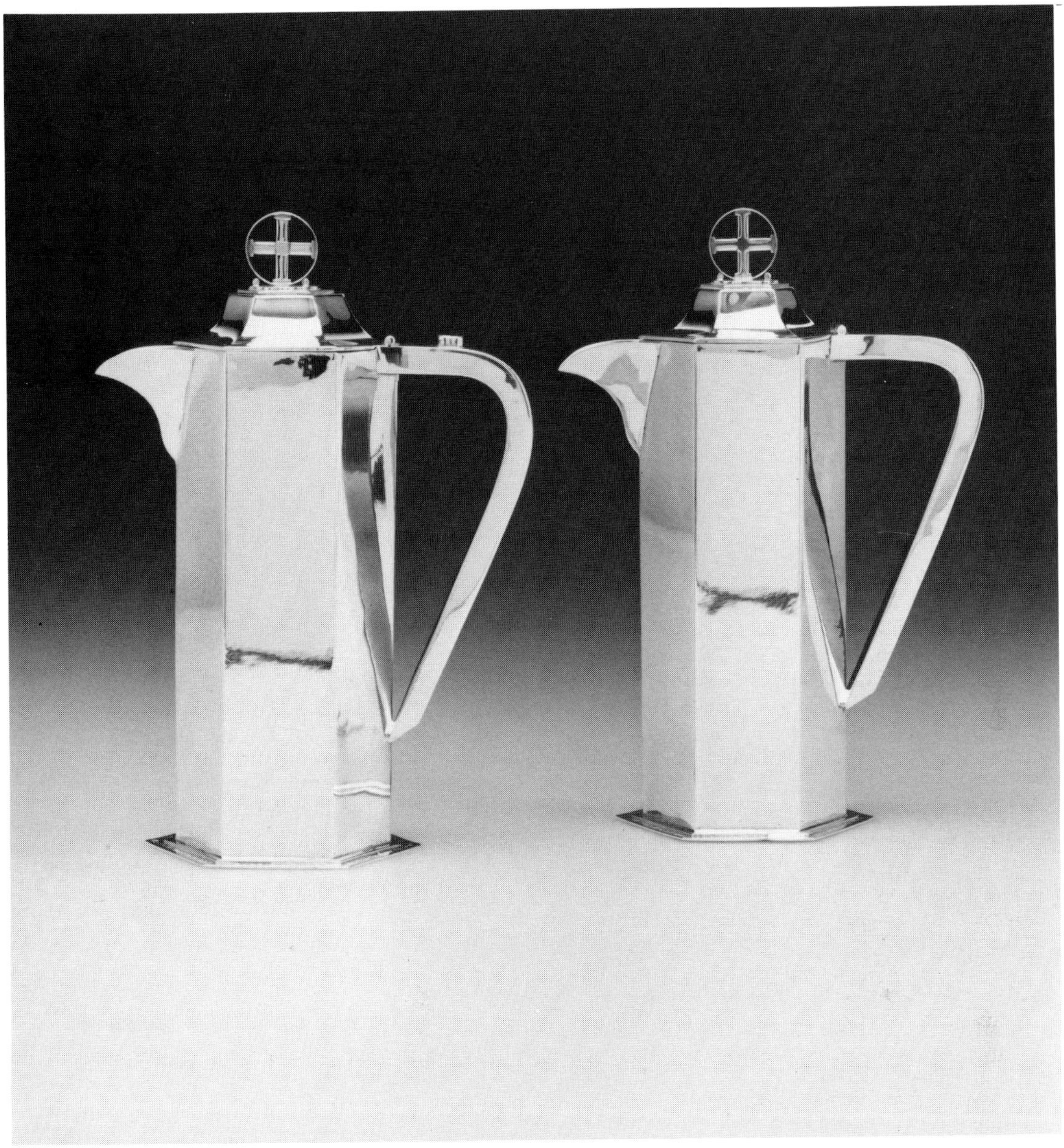

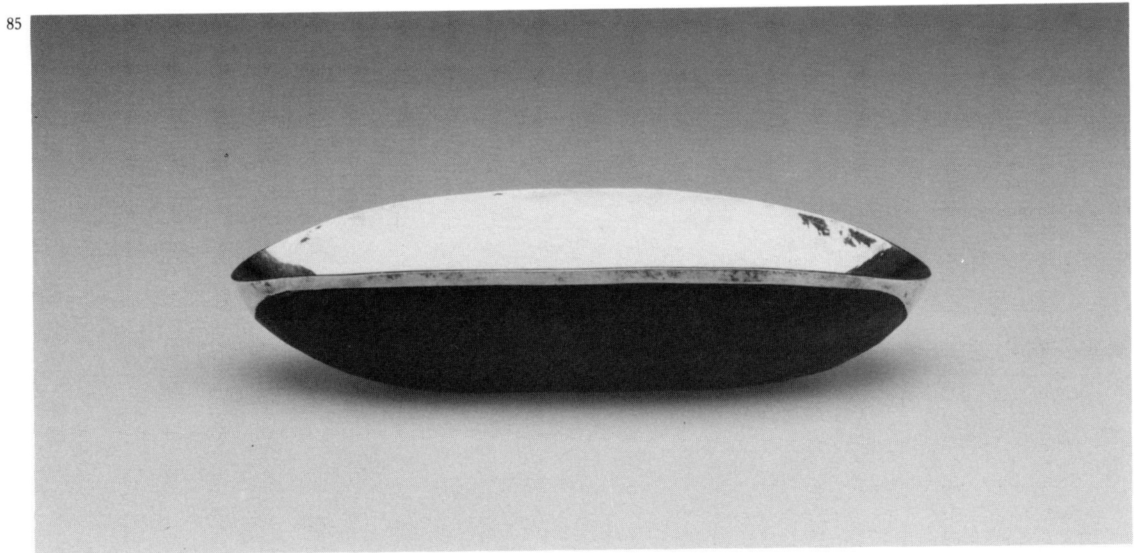

85

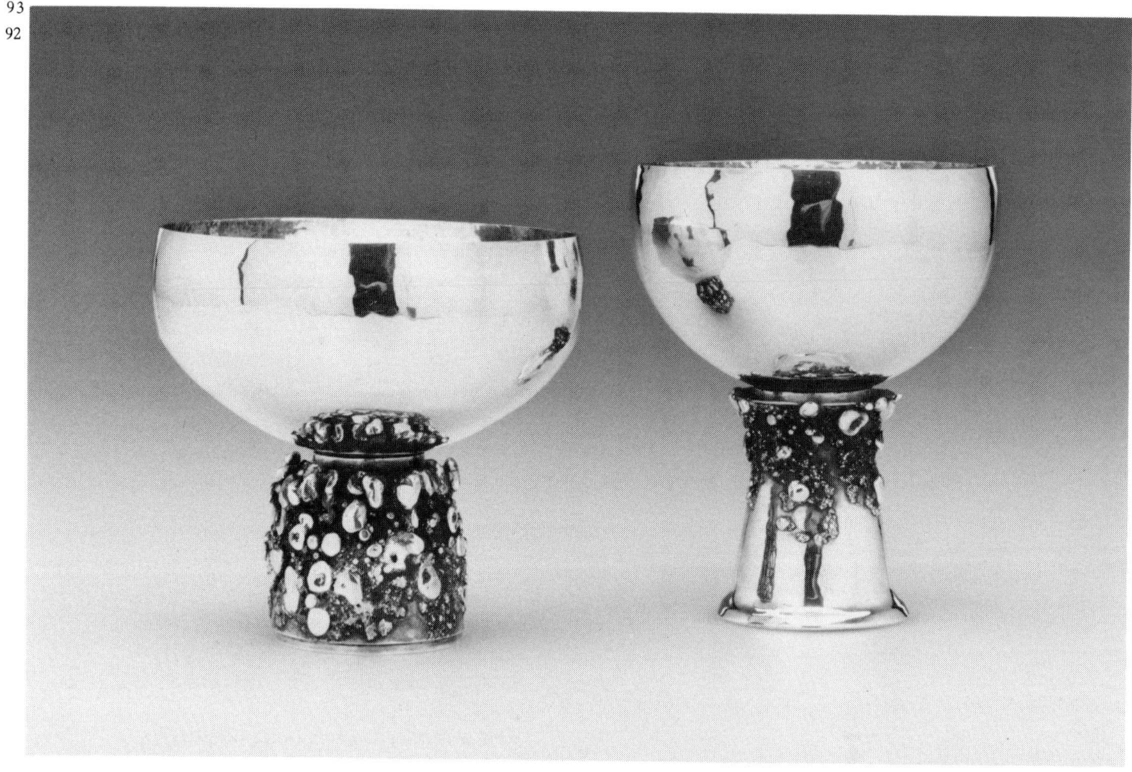

93
92

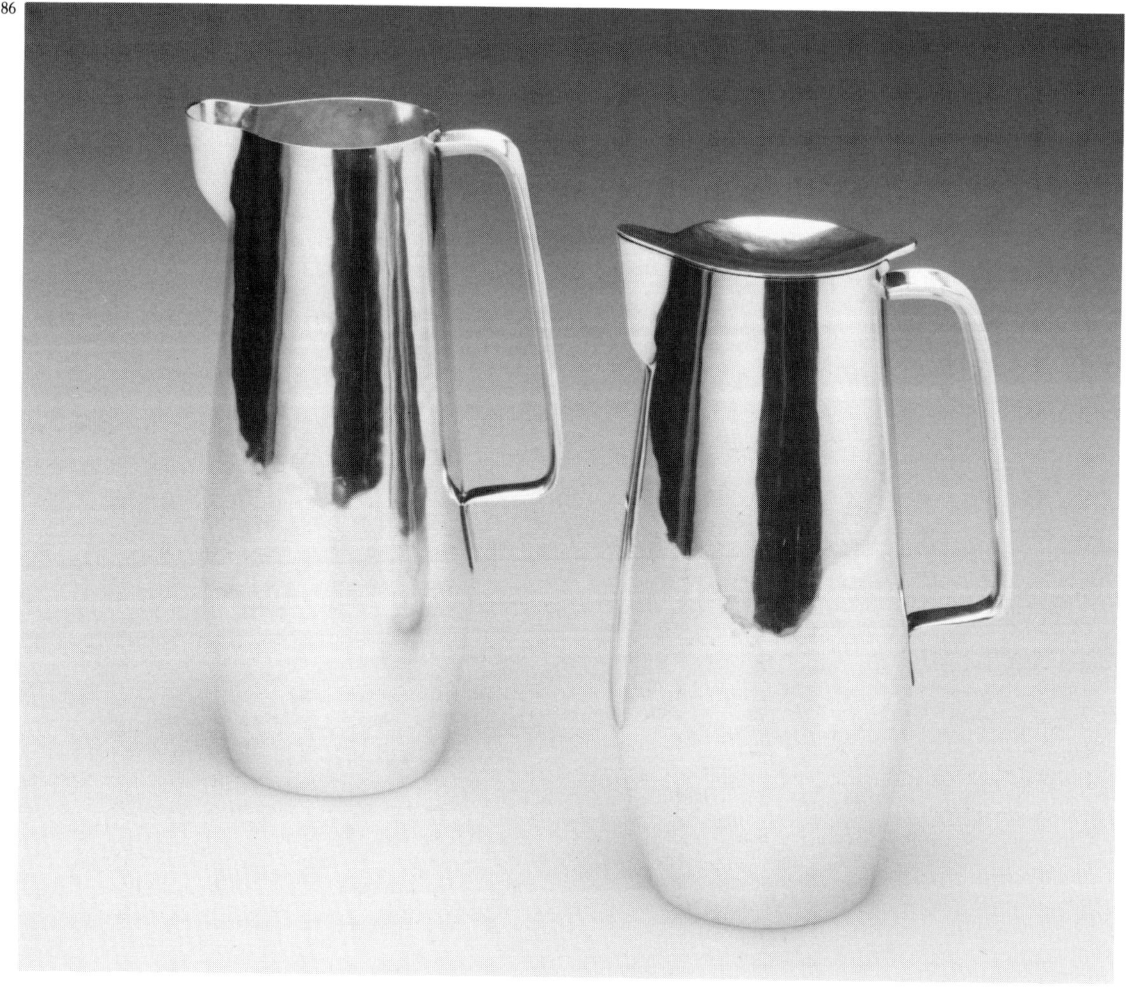

86

horizontally at the rim and turns to rejoin the
lower part of the body at a sharp angle. The handle
of the wine cruet is set with a garnet.

Ernest Fries—Melbourne
B.West Germany 1934 arr.1959

81. CHALICE AND PATEN
1966
Silver-gilt, enamel
Chalice h.26 d.15
Paten d.17.5
Inscribed: 'God is Love. The McCormick Family
1966'
Holy Trinity Anglican Cathedral, Wangaratta,
Victoria

The exterior surface of the bowl is enamelled,
while the interior and the rim are silver-gilt. The
silver-gilt knop, composed of a stylized crown of
thorns, is attached to the cylindrical stem which
flares into a trumpet foot.
    The circular paten is slightly dished.

82. CIBORIUM
1966
Silver-gilt, enamel
H.22.5 d.14.5
Inscribed: 'A.M.D.G. God is Love. The McCormick
Family 1966'
Holy Trinity Anglican Cathedral, Wangaratta,
Victoria

The bowl, enamelled to represent netting, rests on
a convex stem which flares into a trumpet foot.
The conical cover is surmounted by a finial in the
form of a fish.

83. CROZIER
c.1974
Silver
H.196
Lent by His Grace, The Most Reverend Thomas F.
Little, Archbishop of Melbourne
Literature: Rogan 1976, p.23, cat.211

The silver crozier, with a pronounced hammered
surface, is in the form of a shepherd's crook. The
cast figure of Christ on the cross is attached to the
upper part of the staff.

84. PECTORAL CROSS
c.1974
Silver
L.12.3 w.8
Lent by His Grace, The Most Reverend Thomas F.
Little, Archbishop of Melbourne

The cross, with irregularly shaped arms, incor-
porates the modelled figure of Christ with arms
raised.

85. CHALICE AND PATEN
1975
Silver-gilt, silver, wood
Chalice h.6 l.28
Port Keats Catholic Church, Northern Territory
Note: Chalice and paten made for the first
Aboriginal Catholic priest

The chalice is a carved wooden bowl of coolamon
shape lined with silver-gilt.
    The paten is a carved wooden bowl of coolamon
shape inlaid with a flat silver wire around its rim.

Helge Larsen and Darani Lewers—Sydney
Larsen b.Denmark 1929 arr.1961
Lewers b.1936

86. WINE AND WATER EWERS
1967
Silver
H.22.3 and 21.5
Inscribed: Unlidded 'IN MEMORY OF A. HAND
H.M.E. BERTHA LOVE The gift of M.C.
MUTTON, C.J. LOVE, AND THEIR
FRIENDS' Lidded 'THE GIFT OF ST. MARK'S,
DARLING POINT'
Wentworth Memorial Church, Sydney

Each of the ewers has a tall spouted body with the
point of maximum curvature at one third of its
height. The wine ewer has a flat lid shaped to accommodate the spout and tilted upwards to create a
thumbrest. The handle is of U-shape section, with
the upper surface concave.

Hans Arkeveld—Perth
B.Holland 1942 arr.1952

87. PROCESSIONAL/ALTAR CROSS
1968
Bronze, aluminium
H.122 w.25.4
St Dennis Catholic Church, Joondanna, Western
Australia

A bronze figure of the crucified Christ is attached
to a plain aluminium cross.

Moitre Kenwrick—Adelaide
B.1922

88. BAPTISMAL EWER
1968
Silver
H.32
Pulteney Grammar School, Adelaide

The body of the ewer is in two sections meeting at
a sharp angle near the conical foot. The neck, with
beak-shaped spout, is defined by a raised band at
the rim and at the juncture with the body. The
domed cover is surmounted by an encircled cross
finial. The handle has a vertical barley-twist hand-
grip attached by a scroll to the rim of the body.

Albion—Melbourne
(1946–1979)

89. CROZIER
c.1968
Silver-gilt, ivory, electroplate
H.188
Lent by His Grace, The Most Reverend Francis
Patrick Carroll, Archbishop of Canberra and
Goulburn

The head of the crozier, in silver-gilt, is in the form
of a fish, the tail curving inward to join the head.
The curving body encloses an anchor. Below the
crook is a cylindrical knop in ivory. The
electroplated shaft is in two parts, annulated at
their juncture.

Robert Baines—Melbourne
B.1949

90. COMMUNION SERVICE
1969–73
Silver, silver-gilt, enamel
Chalice h.21.6 w.11.6
Paten w.15
Flagon h.26.3 w.12.3
Bread box h.9.3 w.15.8
All Saints' Anglican Church, Greensborough,
Victoria

The bowl of the chalice has a circular base, rising
to a four-sided rim, and is set on an integrated
stem and foot tapering irregularly upwards from a
lozenge-shaped section. The foot is inset with
irregular enamel panels.
  The four-sided, dish-shaped paten has a foot rim.
  The shallow box is of lozenge section tapering
towards the foot and towards the top of the lid.
This is surmounted by a tall finger-grip with an
enamel panel set into the top.
  The body of the flagon is a tapering four-sided
form of lozenge section, which extends into an
angular spout. The cover is surmounted by a
pointed angular thumbrest and is inset with two
enamel panels.

John Howard—Melbourne
B.1935

91. CIBORIUM
1972
Silver
H.29
Victorian College, Burwood Campus

The bowl rests on a cylindrical stem. The cylindrical knop has a central band of openwork composed of two rows of conjoined U-motifs. The
same openwork band decorates the vertical edge of
the foot which rests on a circular base. The cover is
surmounted by a cross finial.

Eric Carr—Perth
B.Alexandria 1936 arr.1949

92. CHALICE
1972
Silver
H.15.4 d.12.5
Lent by Reverend Christopher Ross, O.S.M., Perth

The bowl rests on a tapering cylindrical stem
spreading to a foot with an everted rim. The knop
is delineated by an irregular oxidized surface below
a projecting collar near the juncture with the bowl.

93. CIBORIUM
1972
Silver
H.13.3 d.14.2
Lent by Reverend Christopher Ross, O.S.M., Perth

The bowl of the ciborium rests on a short
cylindrical stem with an irregular oxidized surface.

Marcus Skipper—Eltham, Victoria
B.1950

94. PROCESSIONAL CROSS
c.1974
Silver, wood
H.228 w.32
Inscribed: 'To the Glory of God in Memory of Ethel
and Harry Bracher. O.B. 1972 & 1974 Given by
their Family'
St Mark's Anglican Church, Camberwell, Victoria

The wooden cross has cast silver terminals applied
to the arms; those on the upper arms incorporate a
scrolling foliate motif whereas that of the lower
arm depicts a stylized lion. A cast silver cruciform
panel with central roundel incorporating scrolling
motif is applied at the intersection of the arms. The
cross is mounted over a silver ferrule. The wooden
staff has a large compressed spherical knop in silver
and a silver tip.

95. VERGER'S WAND
c.1974
Silver, wood
H.93.2 w.9
Inscribed: 'to the Glory of God in MEMORY OF
DORIS BAXTER 1900–1974'
St Mark's Anglican Church, Camberwell, Victoria

The cast silver cross, with oxidized highlights, has
an octagonal panel depicting a stylized lion at the
intersection of its arms. The cross is mounted on a
silver knop above a silver ferrule on a wooden staff.

John Campbell—Adelaide
B.1948

96. CHALICE AND PATEN
1981
Silver, gold, silver-gilt, diamonds
Chalice h.15.7 d.9.9

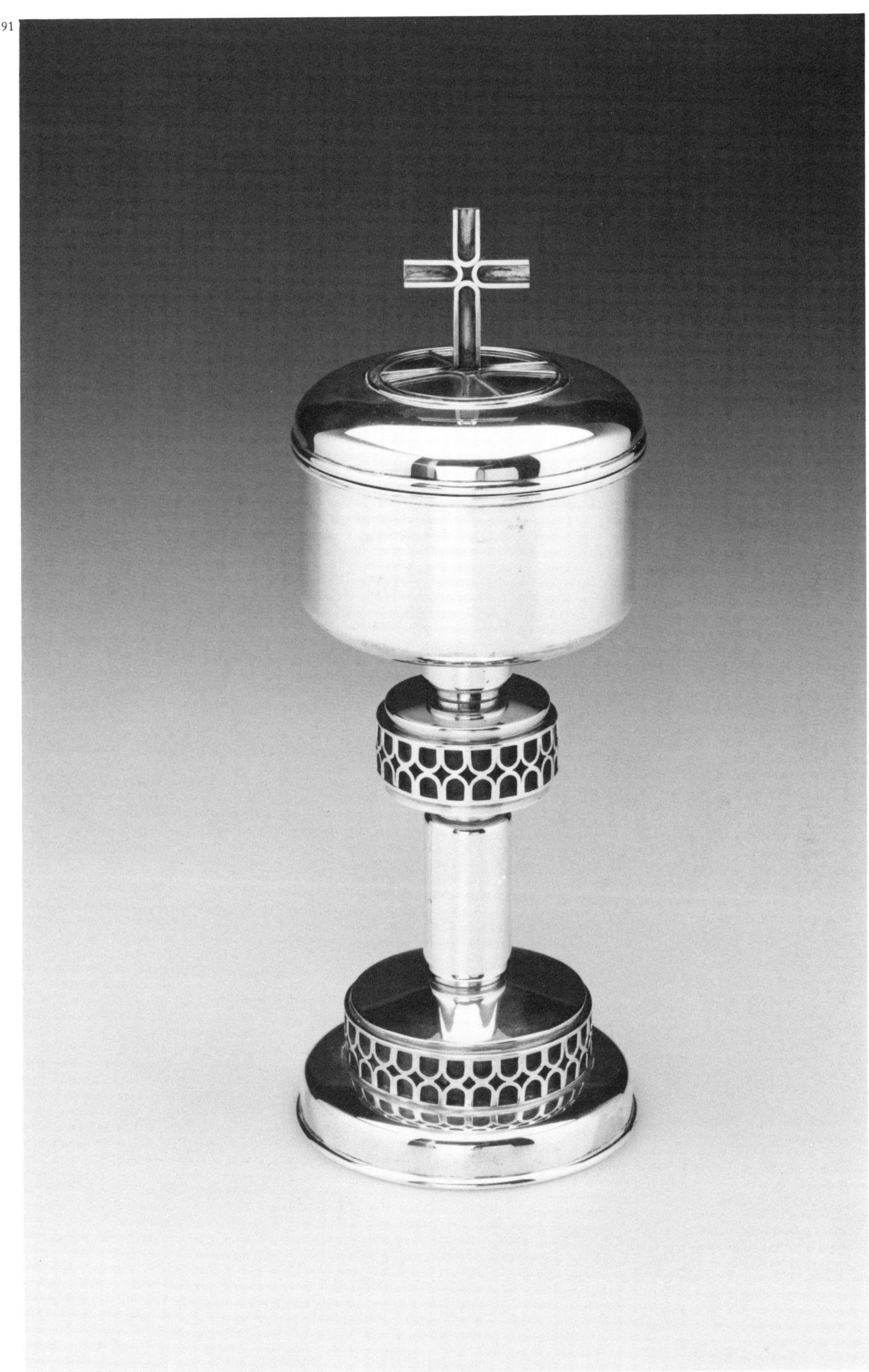

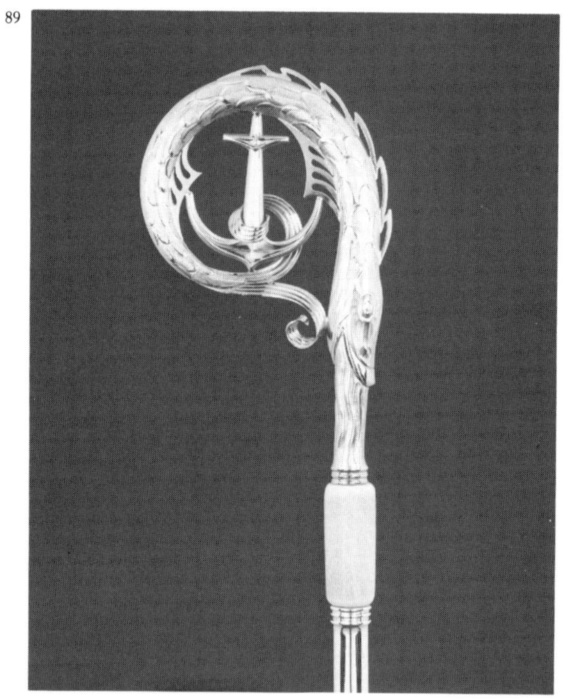

89

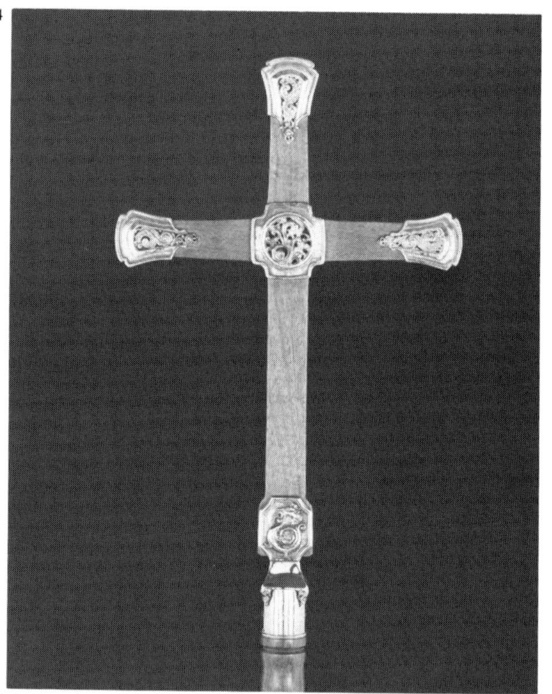

94

88

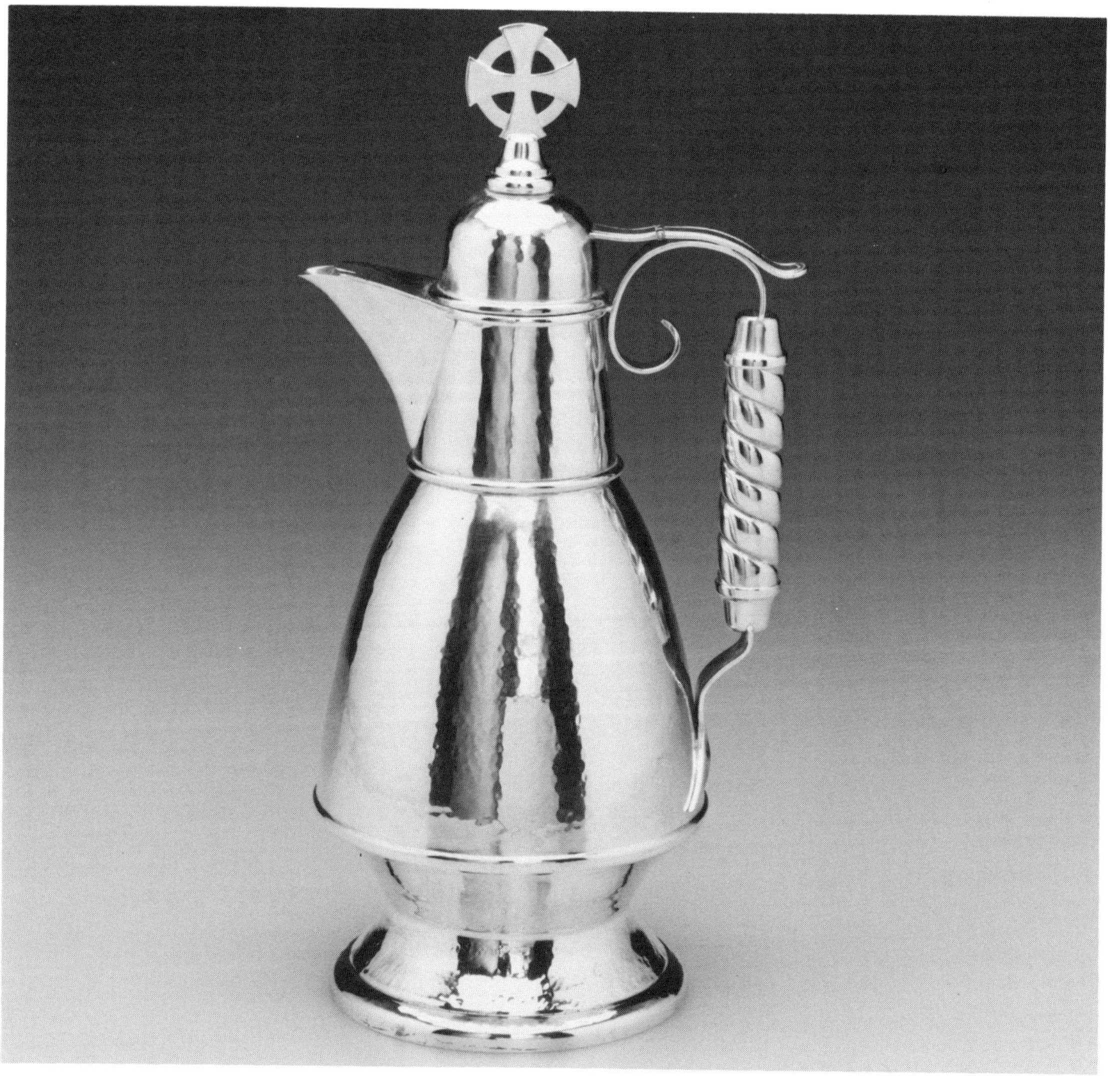

Paten d.14.9
Lent by The Reverend Gary Priest, Bunbury,
Western Australia

The bowl of the chalice rests on a cylindrical stem
flaring into a trumpet foot. The stem is applied
with narrow strips of gold set with stones representing vines and is encircled by a jewelled eternity
ring at its juncture with the bowl. The surface of
the chalice is hammered while the rim of the foot
is cast and applied and is of irregular surface and
outline.

The circular shallow paten has a hammered
surface and the emblem of the Riverina Diocese is
engraved near the rim.

John and Dan Flynn—Kyneton, Victoria
John b.1955
Dan b.1957

97. CHALICE AND PATEN
1984
Silver, silver-gilt, nickel, ebony
Chalice h.17 d.11
Paten d.15
The Church of the Resurrection, Macedon Ranges,
Victoria
Note: The bowl is from the original chalice which
belonged to the Church of the Good Shepherd,
destroyed in the 1983 bushfires.

The bowl has a rough and blackened exterior
surface, plain silver rim and a gilt interior. It rests
on a conical stem, one half formed in wood, the
other as an open silver cross.

The dished paten is chased with a circular
radiating motif.

Ecclesiastical Metalware—Melbourne
Established 1978

98. PASTORAL STAFF
1985
Silver, wood
H.179
Lent by The Right Reverend Peter Hollingworth,
Bishop of the Inner City, Melbourne Diocese

The wooden shepherd's crook has three sections in
silver, one incorporting the knop, one marking a
juncture in the staff and the other incorporating
the tip. Each section has an engraved band representing a crown of thorns. The knop is engraved with
the emblems of St Peter, St Laurence, St John the
Baptist and a fleur-de-lis

Terence County—Melbourne
B.1944

99. PECTORAL CROSS
1985
Gold, silver, amethyst
L.11.5 w.7.5
Inscribed: 'FOR AS MUCH † PETER
HOLLINGWORTH ST MATTHIAS 1985'
Lent by The Right Reverend Peter Holl-
ingworth, Bishop in the Inner City,
Melbourne Diocese

The cross is made in silver and rimmed with
gold. Each of the arms is applied with a wavy
strip of gold engraved to represent thorns.
Three of the arms are applied with an emblem
of a saint—St Peter, St Laurence and St John
the Baptist—while the fourth is applied with a
fleur-de-lis. A faceted amethyst is set at the intersection of the arms.

100. BISHOP'S RING
1985
18c gold, white gold, amethyst
H.3.6
Lent by The Right Reverend Peter Hollingworth, Bishop in the Inner City,
Melbourne Diocese

The gold ring is set with a faceted amethyst,
with the top of the bezel engraved to
represent a crown of thorns. The emblems of
St Peter, St Laurence, St John the Baptist and
a fleur-de-lis, in silver, are applied to the bezel.

BIBLIOGRAPHY

Adams, Bruce. *Hans Arkeveld:Images of a Cagemaker*. Exhibition catalogue. The Art Gallery of Western Australia, Perth, 1984.

Albrecht, Kurt. *Nineteenth Century Australian Gold and Silver Smiths*. Hutchinson, Australia, 1969.

Andrews, Brian. *Gothic in South Australian Churches*. Exhibition catalogue. The Flinders University of South Australia, Adelaide, 1984.

Anson, Peter F. *Fashions in Church Furnishings 1840–1940*. Studio Vista, London, 1965.

Burman, Peter & Nugent, Kenneth (eds). *Prophecy and Vision*. Exhibition catalogue. Committee for Prophecy and Vision, Bristol, 1982.

Bury, Shirley. *Copy or Creation. Victorian Treasures from English Churches*. Exhibition catalogue. Worshipful Company of Goldsmiths and the Victorian Society, London, 1967.

Bury, Shirley et al. *Victorian Church Art*. Exhibition catalogue. Victoria and Albert Museum, London, 1971.

Crawford, Alan et al. *C.R. Ashbee & the Guild of Handicraft*. Exhibition catalogue. Cheltenham Art Gallery and Museum, Cheltenham, 1981.

de Jong, Ursula M. *William Wilkinson Wardell His Life and Work: 1823–1899*. Exhibition catalogue. Department of Visual Arts, Monash University, Clayton, 1983.

Edwards, Geoffrey. *Ernest Fries 1959–1984*. Exhibition catalogue. Otto-Richter-Halle, Würzburg, 1984.

Ewing, G.G. *Exhibition of Ecclesiastical Art*. Exhibition catalogue. St Paul's Cathedral, Melbourne, 1947.

Fries, Ernest. 'Ernest Fries an Autobiography'. *Australian Architecture and Design*, July 1981, pp.22–6.

Gilchrist, James. *Anglican Church Plate*. The Connoisseur and Michael Joseph, London, 1967.

Gray, Anne. *James W.R. Linton 1869–1947*. Exhibition catalogue. The Western Australian Art Gallery, Perth, 1977.

Grimwade, A.G. 'Royal Church Plate of New South Wales'. *The Connoisseur* cxix, 504, June 1947, pp.100–02.

Hawkins, J.B. *Australian Silver 1800–1900*. National Trust of Australia (N.S.W.), Sydney, 1973.

'Royal Presentation Silver with an Australian History'. *The Australasian Antique Collector*. 20th edn, 1980, pp.78–81.

Hodges, F.N. 'Australian Goldsmiths'. Unpublished manuscript. Victoria, c.1970.

Landau, Tyrone. *William Butterfield 1814–1900 Pioneer of High Victorian Gothic Revival Architecture*. Exhibition catalogue. Fischer Fine Art, London, 1982.

Moloney, Parker. *Church Building, Its Furnishing and Uses A Doctrinal Analysis*. Heritage Books, Dickson, 1982.

Moore, William. *The Story of Australian Art*. Vol. II. Angus & Robertson Limited, Sydney, 1934.

Oman, Charles. *English Church Plate 597–1830*. Oxford University Press, London, 1957.

Rodriquez, Judith. 'The Legend of Emily Hope'. *Lip* 8, 1984, pp.94–9.

Rogan, John P. *Australian Gold and Silver 1820–1976*. Exhibition catalogue. The National Gallery of Victoria Women's Association, Melbourne, 1976.

Semmens, Kelman. *Andor Meszaros*. The Hawthorn Press, Melbourne, 1972.

White, James F. *The Cambridge Movement : The Ecclesiologists and the Gothic Revival*. Cambridge University Press, Cambridge, 1962.